THE RESTORATION of *Priesthood*

A CALL TO HOLINESS

GUILLERMO MALDONADO

Our Mission
Called to bring the supernatural power of God to this generation.

The Restoration of Priesthood
Guillermo Maldonado

First Edition: June 2018

ISBN: 978-1-59272-778-0

All rights reserved by Ministerio Internacional El Rey Jesus
(King Jesus International Ministry).

This publication may not be reproduced, altered (in whole or part), archived in any electronic system nor transmitted by any electronic, mechanical (including photocopying or recording devices) or stored in any information storage retrieval system, or in any other manner, without the previous written permission by the author. Unless otherwise indicated, all Scripture quotations are taken from the New King James Version, © 1979, 1980, 1982, 1984 by Thomas Nelson, Inc. Used by permission. Scripture quotations marked (NIV) are taken from the Holy Bible, New International Version®, NIV®, © 1973, 1978, 1984 by the International Bible Society. Used by permission of Zondervan. All rights reserved.

Project Director: Andres Brizuela
Spanish Editors: Jose M Anhuaman - Gloria Zura
Translation: Jessica L. Galarreta - Adriana Mangual
Cover Design: Juan Salgado

Category: Spiritual Growth

King Jesus International Ministry
14100 SW 144th Ave. Miami, FL 33186
Ph: 305.382.3171 - Fx: 305.382.3178
Printed in The United States of America

Index

	Introduction	5
1	Priesthood in Crisis	7
2	The Levitical and Melchizedek Priesthoods	23
3	The New Testament Priesthood	35
4	Responsibilities of the Priest	51
5	A Call to Holiness	71

Introduction

GOD HAS GIVEN me the privilege of writing many books, and each one of them has been born of my intimate relationship with God. It is in the midst of prayer that His Spirit gives me revelation and discernment of the times we live and of what Jesus expects from His Church. A while ago, He showed me the pain of His heart caused by the deterioration of the priesthood in homes and in the church. He also showed me the consequences of the lack of a holy priesthood in today's world. The Lord told me, "The priesthood is asleep and must awaken!"

A terrible characteristic of this generation is that it has abandoned its priesthood; it has abdicated its authority and it has completely lost the standards of holiness and purity. Men grow up ignoring their responsibilities as priests. Women have had to take on burdens that are too heavy for them; and this is wearing them out, causing the enemy to gain ground in homes and in the church, producing a negative impact on society.

The desire in God's heart is that the priesthood, like prayer, is restored at every level, in preparation for the second coming of Christ. This generation of priests needs to get out of the lethargy where it has been sunk. It needs to be constantly watching and praying to discern the times we are living and to hear the voice of God. This royal priesthood must assume its responsibility at all levels, to become the prophetic voice of God, to fulfill His will on earth, to restore the fallen altars, to minister worship to the One true God, and to be light in the midst of darkness.

Today, God is raising a remnant of sons and daughters who have not allowed themselves to be contaminated by the system of the world, who live in holiness, consecrated and set apart for His exclusive use. That remnant has assumed its priestly responsibilities and is paving the way for the second coming of the Great King, Jesus Christ, the Son of God.

You are part of that remnant. Wake up and take your place! Only then will God's blessing come upon your house, growth will come to your ministry, and the glory of God will cover the whole earth.

1 | Priesthood in Crisis

GOD IS SOVEREIGN over heaven and earth—both in the spiritual realm and the physical realm. It has always been His plan for human beings to serve as kings and priests in His kingdom, under His rule. God created the first man and woman, Adam and Eve, in His image and likeness. Then He gave them dominion over all the earth, making them kings and priests over creation. (See Genesis 1:26–28.) In the order of creation, God appointed the man to be head of the family and to serve as its "high priest." (See Ephesians 5:22–24; 1 Corinthians 11:7–12.)

After mankind fell, God instituted His plan to redeem humanity. As part of this plan, He called the nation of Israel to represent His kingdom on earth, saying, *"And you shall be to Me a kingdom of priests and a holy nation"* (Exodus 19:6).

Then Christ came to earth as the Messiah and died on the cross to reconcile mankind to God. Since then, all who believe in Him as Lord and Savior are part of the body of Christ, the church, whose purpose is to fulfill God's eternal plan by exercising authority as His kings and priests on earth:

> *But you are a chosen generation, a royal priesthood, a holy nation, His own special people, that you may proclaim the praises of Him who called you out of darkness into His marvelous light.*
> (1 PETER 2:9)

> *To Him who...has made us kings and priests to His God and Father, to Him be glory and dominion forever and ever.*
> (REVELATION 1:5–6)

> *[You] have made us kings and priests to our God; and we shall reign on the earth.* (REVELATION 5:10)

Before we begin to study how priesthood fell into a state of crisis, which will be the main topic of this chapter, let us study what priesthood is from a biblical point of view.

Who Is a Priest?

God's original intention has always been to empower His people so that, through praise and worship, they can develop an intimate relationship with Him; since this is key in the priestly function. *"For every high priest taken from among men is appointed for men in things pertaining to God, that he may offer both gifts and sacrifices for sins".* (Hebrews 5:1). Therefore, in both the Old and New Testaments, the figure of the priest is described as one who offers spiritual sacrifices to God.

People often have misconceptions about what it means to be a true spiritual priest in Christ. This does not require wearing a cassock or abstaining from marriage, as some traditional religions practice. Jesus is the model of the priest of the New Testament. He dressed according to the custom of His time, He walked with the people, saw their needs, shared his joys, cried their losses, rejoiced in their parties, prayed and interceded for them and gave Himself in their favor. That is how He became both the Priest who ministered the sacrifice, and the sacrifice itself. He is the lamb without blemish that blots out the sin of the world (see, for example, Hebrews 9:14; 1 Peter 1:19).

The Priesthood Falls into a Crisis

It is no secret to anyone that the spiritual priesthood is in crisis today, as it has been many times throughout history. However, in order to understand why, we need to go back to Eden, the place where the priesthood crisis began. While it is true that both Adam and Eve had authority given by God to rule over creation, the primacy of authority was entrusted to the man. God gave Adam a kingdom, even before entering into a covenant with him. However, when Adam disobeyed God and agreed, along with Eve, to take Satan's suggestion and eat the fruit of the tree of the knowledge of good and evil, he rebelled against his Creator, and automatically abdicated his authority. In that instant, the priesthood fell into a crisis, and to this day we continue to suffer the consequences of this disobedience.

But it has not always been like this. The primitive church knew how to shake off that sequel of rebellion. For example, the disciples of Jesus, following the model of their Master, performed the priestly function very well. In the same way, they chose good priests to send them to other cities, to exercise a holy priesthood. The Scripture says that no one was there "to be served", but to minister to God and serve the people. However, in modern times the church has lost its focus on the priestly function, it has accommodated to the convenience of the people and has deviated to the point that it no longer fulfills its responsibilities.

One of the direct consequences of this priesthood crisis is the collapse and moral corruption of society. For that reason, it is common to hear people say, "If the priests, pastors, teachers, prophets, apostles, evangelists and Christian leaders can lie, steal, commit adultery, fornicate, divorce, judge, criticize and get angry; then we can do it too". People see in the priesthood crisis a license to lower their own moral standards. When the church weakens its position or is not firm to act in the face of immorality and injustice, it stops making a difference in a society that is expecting to walk under their leadership.

The priesthood is the moral compass of society, and it's the only thing that legitimizes the church.

A generation without an upright priesthood lives in anarchy. In fact, evil and corruption will only be eradicated from a home, a city, nation or church that has an honest priesthood; that will stand firm, present their bodies as a living sacrifice, offer praise and worship, do good to others and present offerings to God. When moral decadence reaches the priesthood, it affects all levels of society. The church will never be legitimized by its charisma, eloquence, education, or powerful preaching and teachings; but it will be by the faithfulness of its priesthood in hearing what God is speaking for this time, and in acting accordingly, with boldness and morality.

Nowadays, the majority of men don't exercise the priesthood that God assigned to them. The reason why the ministry of intercession is full of women is because men have abandoned their priestly function, and now those ministries are qualified or seen as feminine. The truth is that, faced with the desertion of men –in other words, since men abdicated their authority in Eden–, women have had to assume functions that they are not supposed to be responsible for. As a result, we see a lot of women who are overwhelmed, tired and burnt out, because they are carrying burdens that don't correspond with God's design for them.

The problem in modern society is that men want to be kings without being priests; they want to govern, but not serve; much less that we speak to them about seeking God. But in the kingdom of God things don't work that way. It is true men have been called to be kings and priests. However, a king is someone who first marches to war, who guides his army in battles; and a priest is one who presents offerings and sacrifices to God. In the priesthood of Melchizedek and in the priesthood of the Levites, we see a pattern: all those who exercised the priesthood were men; not women. And don't misunderstand me; a woman can fulfill priestly functions, but the one who is called to be the high priest in the house is the man.

In the Bible, the priesthood has always been a responsibility of the men.

Causes of the priesthood crisis

We can identify many causes; however, there are four main reasons why there is a crisis in the priesthood:

- **The corruption of character**

    Throughout the Scriptures we read that the strongest reprimands from God were always against false prophets and corrupt priests. *"For the lips of a priest should keep knowledge, and people should seek the law from his mouth; For he is the messenger of the Lord of hosts. But you have departed from the way; You have caused many to stumble at the law. You have corrupted the covenant of Levi, "Says the Lord of hosts"* (Malachi 2:7-8).

    In the times of Malachi, the priesthood had corrupted in such a way, that instead of showing the people the way of the Lord, they made them stumble. A corrupt priesthood corrupts a family, a church, a nation; the people lose their respect for them and God says: *"Therefore I also have made you contemptible and base Before all the people, because you have not kept My ways but have shown partiality in the law."* (Malachi 2:9).

    A man that doesn't exercise his priesthood in his family lacks the moral authority to guide his children according to biblical principles and values. A nation without priesthood cannot live under standards of justice and morality. If the priesthood violates the laws of the nation, the country is in trouble, and under a curse. *"And it shall be: like people, like priest. So I will punish them for their ways, And reward them for their deeds"* (Hosea 4:9). This means that, when the priesthood falls, the people receive the punishment of their corruption; the church loses authority and stops being a light.

    No society collapses if its priesthood has not collapsed first.

Morality standards have been degraded by the priesthood itself, and society has become accustomed to living that way. The priesthood is entirely questionable; their behavior is as corrupt as anyone's. And the difference between the righteous and the unrighteous, between the pure and the impure, between the good and the bad is negligible. Those called to exercise priesthood, lie, get drunk and commit fraud, just like everyone else. There are people who, as they are telling us something, we know beforehand that they will not keep their word; there is no reason to believe them, because they have the intention of not complying; they make promises they soon forget; they don't honor their word, not even in a legal document. That is why, in modern society, just as it happens in the church in these times, people say one thing and do another, but most of the times they just don't do anything.

When justice and righteousness are lacking in the priesthood, integrity loses its meaning in society.

A clear example of priestly corruption were Eli's sons, who *"... were corrupt; they did not know the Lord... Therefore, the sin of the young men was very great before the Lord, for men abhorred the offering of the Lord... Now Eli was very old; and he heard everything his sons did to all Israel, and how they lay with the women who assembled at the door of the tabernacle of meeting"* (1 Samuel 2:12, 17, 22). These priests sinned and caused the people to sin.

Many priests in these days are not very different. They preach messages that justify people's licentious lifestyle, because they live in ungodliness and without the fear of God themselves. They deny or distort truth in the name of the hyper-grace message, which states that, if we are saved by grace, we can live as we want. This has caused people to conform to sin, instead of allowing God to transform them until they reflect the character of Christ. When someone feels comfortable with their sin, they don't change. Likewise, a priest cannot ask the people to be righteous, if their personal life is not an example of rectitude and morality.

No priest has the moral authority to rebuke that which they practice.

If we are joined with that which doesn't come from God, we will not be able to rebuke it. Jesus told the scribes: *"How can Satan cast out Satan?"* (Mark 3:23). Sadly, the priesthood has departed from God's righteousness and holiness; and that's why they cannot condemn sin, because it has become a part of them. Thus, each time the church tries to raise its voice in society; it is not heard nor respected, because corruption screams so loud that it doesn't allow others to hear what it has to say. It is true that there are still things that all of us struggle with, because we are still growing in the Lord and we make mistakes. However, this is different from openly living a life of sin and iniquity.

Truth and justice must be our life standards.

How can we tell someone not to lie, or commit injustices or to not steal, if those who are supposed to set the example lie, steal and are unjust? In that moment, moral authority is lost. When someone tells a lie, they need to keep lying to protect themselves; but the truth is still one and it cannot be twisted. There is no such thing as a half-truth, or a second version of the truth.

The Bible says: *"Justice is turned back, and righteousness stands afar off; for truth is fallen in the street, and equity cannot enter"* (Isaiah 59:14). Truth is fallen in the street? Equity cannot enter? What is the Lord telling us? Here God is showing us the decadence of morality. The average people would say that nothing is bad and everything is valid or acceptable, "as long as it makes them happy". That is compromising the truth in order to feel good! If we allow this, we will lose the authority God has given us. If a priest is not capable of making a difference in the society where he lives, then he is not suitable either to represent the people before God, nor can he confront the enemy to defend his family or to snatch back from him the territories he has stolen from them. These territories can be for example, the finances, their children's life, their ministry, etc.

> **Every time Israel went to war without the guidance of their priesthood, they lost the battles.**

Our generation is seeing the increase of immorality among the priests of the catholic church and other denominations, which has made itself evident in the sexual abuse of children, rape of women, homosexual or adulterous relations, among other things they haven't admitted. Of course, there's also moral corruption in the protestant Christian church, for example, scandals of fraud, adultery, divorces, bad use of the tithes and abuse of authority. All these have led to society marginalizing the church; because the priesthood has covered up sin, instead of recognizing it, repenting and allowing God to transform them.

The priesthood has been corrupted to such a level, that there are denominations who ordain homosexual men and women to ministry, or hold weddings of same sex couples, disregarding God's command (see, for example, Leviticus 18:22). They even allow worship leaders who are openly homosexuals on the altar; and I don't have anything against those people, because I understand that God loves the sinner, but abhors their sin. For all these things, the church has lost authority to show society how to live a righteous life. Before, if a politician had the support of a pastor, people understood that this man was righteous and respectable; today, they do not care to listen to the voice of the church.

▪ The neglecting of the priesthood

The western culture has imposed the idea that spiritual matters or anything related to God are "women's things". As a result, the one who prays at home is the woman; the one who goes to church and educates the children in the fear of God is the woman; the one who fasts, gives offerings and presents sacrifices to the Lord is the woman. God entrusted the priesthood to men; but, like Adam, men have abandoned or neglected their holy call. Hence, the women have had to assume the priestly responsibilities in the home; a task for which God did not commission them.

Furthermore, divorces leave more and more families without their priest; and the men who stay married get used to working hard all day, and then getting home to just sit in front of the television. They believe their only responsibility is to be providers; and for that reason, they have a full-time job and several part time jobs, to be able to cover all their home's needs. So, the devil makes sure he keeps this kind of men working a lot and earning little, so that their needs don't allow them to take on their function as priests. Meanwhile, the role of raising the children has fallen on the women. For that reason, many children only have a female point of reference, and from dad they only receive abandonment and neglect, a bad example and a lack of love.

■ Matriarchy and male chauvinism

When God had to expel Adam and Eve from Eden because of their sin, he explained the consequences that it would bring. *"To the woman He said: ...Your desire shall be for your husband, and he shall rule over you."* (Genesis 3:16). That is why; the enemy has always attacked men's priesthood with a spirit of male chauvinism, but also with a spirit of matriarchy. Male chauvinism is a distortion of priesthood, by which the man, instead of exercising authority through love, service and example, subjugates and hurts his whole family. His children fear him, but don't respect him. His wife obeys him, but is mistreated, as if she was inferior to him.

The matriarchal spirit rises as an opponent of male chauvinism. Due to the man abdicating his authority in Eden, the woman has taken the place that belonged to him as spiritual authority and head of the family. However, it's important to emphasize that, even though we are all priests, we are not all priestly heads. While we all have spiritual authority, not all of us have the same authority; and even though the ministries are not given according to gender, the man has been assigned the exercise of the priesthood in the family.

■ Ignorance

So, we see that as a consequence of the points mentioned above, there is a generation that doesn't know what priesthood is. They never saw that figure in their homes or their churches. Ignorance is a weapon the enemy uses to draw people away from the truth. Nowadays, priesthood is a matter that has been forgotten; it is not taught in seminars, biblical institutes, or in discipleships. For the same reason, even if men want to assume their priestly role, they don't know how to do it, and end up suffering the consequences of disobeying God, *"...though he does not know it, yet he is guilty and shall bear his iniquity"* (Leviticus 5:17).

Two kinds of ignorance

There are two kinds of ignorance in human beings: The involuntary ignorance and the voluntary ignorance.

- *Involuntary ignorance*

Nobody chooses this kind of ignorance, but it inevitably comes as a result of not having been exposed to the truth. Today, society worries more about children preparing to compete in the labor market, than about teaching them moral principles and educating them to exercise the priesthood established by God. Most of churches don't teach Christians their priestly duties, nor do they instruct them to be good sons and daughters, husbands and wives, and parents. However, God is raising a new generation, and is restoring men to fulfill their priestly functions, both in their family, and at church and the government.

The Bible shows us the history of King Josiah, who began reigning over Judah when he was only eight years old. One of his greatest accomplishments was to restore the priesthood of Israel. The reforms that he undertook during his kingdom are described in the second book of Chronicles. His predecessor, King Amon, Josiah's father, had corrupted the people by building altars to honor pagan gods, but when Josiah ascended to the throne, he started removing all those altars, he destroyed the statues and ordered the false priests out of the temple, in order to restore the true priesthood of Jehovah.

What produced such a radical change? As he was rebuilding the temple, the King found the book of law, of whose existence he had no knowledge, and started reading it. Then, God brought conviction of sin, and Josiah was quick to repent. Immediately, the King ordered the people to obey the law of the Lord. *"The king went up to the house of the Lord, with all the men of Judah and the inhabitants of Jerusalem—the priests and the Levites, and all the people, great and small. And he read in their hearing all the words of the Book of the Covenant which had been found in the house of the Lord. Then the king stood in his place and made a covenant before the Lord, to follow the Lord, and to keep His commandments and His testimonies and His statutes with all his heart and all his soul, to perform the words of the covenant that were written in this book"* (2 Chronicles 34:30-31).

Today, the Lord is lifting up a generation of young leaders, with the fear of God and revelation of their functions and authority as priests. They are leaders who love and take care of their wives, who raise their children in obedience to the Father and are of influence in society. Those modern Josiah's accept their calling, live in holiness and raise up a banner of justice on the earth, to lead the remnant that will see the second coming of our great High Priest, Jesus Christ.

- *Voluntary ignorance*

There is another type of ignorance that is worse than the previous one, and it is chosen voluntarily. The Scripture says that *"...that servant who knew his master's will, and did not prepare himself or do according to his will, shall be beaten with many stripes. But he who did not know, yet committed things deserving of stripes, shall be beaten with few..."* (Luke 12:47-48).

Here, God clearly warns us that ignorance is not an excuse nor it exempts us from sin. When He demands men to exercise their priesthood, it is because He considers it a serious matter. That is why, the Lord said: *"My people are destroyed for lack of knowledge. Because you have rejected knowledge, I also will reject you from being priest for Me; because you have forgotten the law of your God, I also will forget your children"* (Hosea 4:6). God wanted Israel to be a nation of priests, but they chose to ignore the Lord. The same thing happens in our time and the consequences this brought in those days are the same it brings today: people lose their marriages, the people are defeated, their houses are destroyed, and their children fall trapped in vices, crime and depression. Everything because their parents didn't know how to be priests in their home and preferred to ignore the voice of God.

> **The greatest stronghold the enemy has lifted in the mind of man is ignorance.**

Nowadays, there are no excuses for remaining in ignorance. The resources are available, and the Holy Spirit is willing to assist us and guide us to all truth.

ACTIVATION

Beloved reader, the challenge is on your side. I challenge you today to stand up and face the reality of your priesthood. If you recognize you have not been the priest that your family needs; if you have abdicated as a priest and handed over the reins of your house to your wife; if the spirit of male chauvinism or matriarchy are stopping you from being a priest according to God's design; if you are corrupted by sin and immorality or you simply ignore what it is to be a priest, or what your functions are, and how to exercise your priesthood; then, God is calling you now!

Join me and repeat the following prayer out loud:

"Beloved Heavenly Father, I come before Your presence because I feel I have been confronted. Now I understand I am not the priest You expect me to be. I have corrupted my priesthood and I don't have the respect of my family. I have let myself be dominated by male chauvinism and matriarchy; I don't know how to be that priest who gives direction to his children, who makes his wife feel loved, secure and who respects her husband. Before I didn't know what it is to be a priest, or its true functions. Today, with all my heart, I ask you for forgiveness. I sincerely repent and renounce to everything that has stopped me from exercising my priesthood. I make a commitment to get out of ignorance, to take corruption out of my life and become a priest through whom the priesthood of Christ will be able to flow upon my wife, my children, my house and every sphere in my life. I give you thanks Lord, in the name of Jesus! Amen!"

TESTIMONIES

JOSHUA GREW WITHOUT A father and without God, in a home where priesthood was completely absent. This is his testimony:

"I know a lot of young people can identify with my history because it happens often. I grew without a father. I always lacked his example; someone to follow or to look like. My life was a chaos, and it was founded on rebellion; I didn't have identity and I didn't know the love of God. I didn't respect the rules; I was disrespectful to my mother, my stepfather, to whoever. My rebellion was such, that my parents were about to throw me out of the house, believing that I would never change. I lived depressed, sunk in my addiction to drugs; I spent hours drinking alcohol, alone, in my room. I felt empty and lost. I would do whatever it took to calm the pain in my heart. Drugs helped me for a moment, but soon after I started feeling that enormous emptiness again. I didn't see a way out of my situation! However, today I can say that the only answer is Jesus. But it wasn't easy; He had to go after me. Thanks to Him, now I'm a living testimony of what His love can do. After so many nights of emptiness and loneliness, now I feel like a new person. God restored my relationship with my stepfather, my mother and my younger brother. I had always hoped to hear my mother say, 'I love you', but since our relationship was broken, she had never been able to do it, until now. I hadn't talked to my stepfather for five years, but now we have a good relationship. God even restored the relationship with my biological father, who found me through Facebook. Today, my younger brother sees me as an example, and has decided to give his life to Christ; wants to be part of the vision of our church because he sees the fruit in my life and in my relationships. God brought me home and has allowed me to bring my family with me, so we can serve Him together".

It is impacting how God can change a person's life just by having an encounter with his Father's love, which is reflected in men who know how to exercise their priesthood!

"My name is Kelly. Before coming to God, everything was different; we lived a disorganized life and with many needs. I lived a big part of my childhood in the midst of chaos. I remember what I felt those days when we didn't have a home or stability, because they always evicted us from where we lived, again and again! Actually, for a couple of months we had to live, my family and I (eight people), in a hotel room. My parents' relationship was so bad that it came to the brink of divorce. My father, who had already left the house, met with my mother at a restaurant, with the divorce papers in his hand. In the restaurant, they run into an acquaintance of them, who had gone through a great financial crisis. They had even seen him riding a bike to work. However, he now had a car, and he had changed a lot. My parents asked him what he had done, and he told them that God had transformed him and now he had a new and blessed life in Christ. That day their lives changed completely. My parents decided to do the same and went with him to church. In only one service, God transformed their lives forever. That same day, Apostle Maldonado gave them a prophetic word for their marriage and everything changed! The impartation was so radical that today, they are an example for me and my siblings, because they are true priests of the kingdom of God. Now, we walk under open heavens; my father's business has been blessed, our finances were restored, and we even have our own house in an excellent city area. We can travel and join our Apostle in his missionary trips. We all serve God in different areas. We always give the glory to Him for what He did in our family. The mantle of priesthood that is upon our church, made the difference in our home. My parents and their commitment to God have formed me and changed the way I approach Him. Jesus restored the priesthood in our home, and I will always be thankful to Him. Now, in my house you can feel His presence and that is priceless. Thank you, Abba!"

2 | The Levitical and Melchizedek Priesthoods

BIBLICAL HISTORY SHOWS us that, since ancient times, man has exercised priestly functions. (See, for example, Genesis 15:9; 26:25; 28:18; 33:20). In those days, it was not only the patriarchs who used to build altars and offer sacrifices, as we can see in the case of Cain and Abel (Genesis 4:4) and of Noah (Genesis 8:20). In fact, throughout the Old Testament we can observe two types of priesthood: the Levitical priesthood, instituted according to the order of Aaron (see Exodus 29:9), which began after the deliverance of Israel from their captivity in Egypt; and the priesthood according to the order of Melchizedek, to which the books of Genesis, Psalms and Hebrews make reference.

In this chapter we will analyze these two types of priesthood and we will observe their remarkable differences.

The Levitical Priesthood

Both the Levitical and Melchizedek priesthoods have ties to Abram, later called Abraham. God called Abraham from an idolatrous family that lived in Ur of the Chaldeans, and asked him to leave everything to go to the place that He would show him. In return, He promised him: *"...I will make you a great nation; I will bless you and make your name great; and you shall be a blessing. I will bless those who bless you, and I will curse him who curses you; and in you all the families of the earth shall be blessed."* (Genesis 12:2-3). Abraham's promised son, Isaac, was born when Abraham was one hundred years old and Sarah, his wife, had reached 90 years of age. The faith of Abraham to wait on God's faithfulness unleashed the fulfillment of all the other promises. Three generations later, the people that had come from the loins of this patriarch multiplied in such a way, that they came to be "numberless."

God had made a covenant with Abraham saying: *"Also I give to you and your descendants after you the land in which you are a stranger, all the land of Canaan, as an everlasting possession; and I will be their God."* (Genesis 17:8) However, on the way to the promised land, the people fell under the Egyptian slavery, and God had to intervene to deliver them. For that, He raised up a new leader, Moses. When they were safe in the desert, the Lord made a new covenant with them and established them as a nation. Israel would be very different from other peoples, because it wouldn't have a king, but would be under God's reign; for it was a nation that was chosen and consecrated for Him. *"You have seen what I did to the Egyptians, and how I bore you on eagles' wings and brought you to Myself. Now therefore, if you will indeed obey My voice and keep My covenant, then you shall be a special treasure to Me above all people; for all the earth is Mine. And you shall be to Me a kingdom of priests and a holy nation..."* (Exodus 19:4-6).

God chose Israel to make it a priestly nation. Therefore, when He told Moses to build the tabernacle, He also gave him instructions on how to separate, anoint and consecrate the priests. Twelve tribes came from Abraham; and the tribe of Levi was chosen specifically for priesthood, with Moses's brother, Aaron, as the high priest. However, the entire nation of Israel became priestly by design, calling and purpose. Each person in the country was a priest, even though only the Levites could exercise the priesthood in the tabernacle. God separated them to Himself; therefore, Israel would be the womb that would conceive the Messiah and High Priest of humanity: Jesus.

The kings of Israel didn't go to war without the word of the prophet and the blessing of the priest.

The priestly call and office

Thus, having a priestly call is not the same as exercising the office of a priest. All of Israel was called to be a priestly nation, but the office was only for the tribe of Levi. In the new covenant, under which we live, we all have a priestly call, but not all of us exercise the office of priests. This does not mean that we become passive believers. If you are a man, who is married or married with children, you must exercise the priesthood actively in your home, praying, presenting offerings to God, serving your family, being an authority over your wife and children. If you are a single mother, you are called by God to exercise the priestly function in your home.

The priesthood of Melchizedek

Melchizedek was a type of Jesus, very superior to Abraham. Of him the Scripture says, *"For this Melchizedek, king of Salem, priest of the Most High God, who met Abraham returning from the slaughter of the kings and blessed him, to whom also Abraham gave a tenth part of all, first being translated "king of righteousness" and then also king of Salem, meaning "king of peace," without father, without mother, without genealogy, having neither beginning of days nor end of life, but made like the Son of God, remains a priest continually. [...] but he whose genealogy is not derived from them received tithes from Abraham and blessed him who had the promises"* (Hebrews 7:1-3, 6).

The first time the Bible mentions the word "priest" is in reference to Melchizedek, who received Abram, after the latter had defeated the kings who had attacked Sodom. In the middle of the battle, Abraham had rescued his nephew Lot and his family, who had been taken captive. *"Then Melchizedek king of Salem brought out bread and wine; he was the priest of God Most High. And he blessed him and said: Blessed be Abram of God Most High, Possessor of heaven and earth"* (Genesis 14:18-19).

A kingdom of priests and kings

Melchizedek blessed Abram because, *"Now beyond all contradiction the lesser is blessed by the better"* (Hebrews 7:7). Although Abram was a legitimate prophet of God, he had to give the tithes to Melchizedek, because he knew he was greater than him; because the latter was a priest and a king. Biblically, Melchizedek is a priestly order, of which Jesus is High Priest (see Hebrews 6:20). It is also the greatest of the priesthoods mentioned in the biblical text.

> **The priesthood of Melchizedek is greater and more powerful, because it requires us to be kings and priests.**

In the New Testament, Jesus is revealed as the King of kings, Lord of lords and High Priest after the order of Melchizedek. Therefore, the Scripture also calls His people *"a royal priesthood"* (see 1 Peter 2:9). What characterizes this priesthood? That it is eternal, because it transcends time, it has no beginning or an end and it encompasses both the Old and the New Testaments. One example of this type of priesthood is King David, who lived in times of the Old Testament, but exercised his priesthood a thousand years before Jesus was born. He reveals and exalts Him in Psalm 22 and 23 as the Good shepherd who takes care and gives His life for His sheep; and in Psalm 24 as the Lord and King who will return for them. However, to understand this we must have revelation of the work of the cross as an eternal event and of the power of the resurrection; because Jesus, sovereign over all the kings of the earth, first had to conquer death, then make us kings and priests for God, His Father (see Revelation 1:5-6).

As kings and priests, we have different levels of authority, which are related to our calling. For example, an apostle has greater authority in the Spirit, as king and priest, because their call is backed by a greater anointing that encompasses vast territories and multitudes of people. Therefore, God gives them access to presidents of nations and other high authorities, so that His voice reaches high spheres through them, and so that they can govern from the spiritual realm with the authority given to them by God. Hence, Scripture reiterates that Jesus *"has made us kings and priests to our God; and we shall reign on the earth."* (Revelation 5:10).

Regarding the anointing to influence governmental spheres, the Bible shows us that several kings were visited in dreams by God, and the Lord revealed to them what they had to do. For example: when Pharaoh dreamed of seven lean and seven fat cows, the Lord sent Joseph, with the anointing of a king and priest, to reveal the meaning of his dream and guide him wisely to save Egypt and the people of God, from the famine that spread throughout the earth. Solomon was another one of the kings visited by God in dreams. *"At Gibeon the Lord appeared to Solomon in a dream by night; and God said, Ask! What shall I give you?"* (1 Kings 3:5). And God gave him wisdom, like no other; and also gave him riches and honor that the young king had not asked.

Hence, when we go before God we should pray as priests and kings, not as beggars. Regardless of whether we hold a high office in the ministry or are new believers, we all have a priestly calling. We must pray in the spirit realm for presidents, prime ministers, kings, and for all who are in eminence – whether we sympathize with them or not –, so that they may have a visitation from God.

Differences between the Levitical and Melchizedek Priesthoods

Having understood the two types of priesthood that God established, let us now see the differences between them:

See the comparative table on the next page

Levitical Priesthood	Melchizedek Priesthood
■ **It was of symbols and shadows** The OT priesthood was only a symbolism of the truth that came with Jesus. Thus, the high priest was the only one who entered the Holy of holies to intercede for the people. (See, for example, Leviticus 16:17; Hebrews 8:4-5).	■ **It is the reality and fullness of the priesthood** Jesus is our high priest, who intercedes for us before the Father. Today, we can all enter the Holy of holies confidently as sons and daughters (see Hebrews 4:15-16).
■ **It was based on rituals** They had to repeat the sacrifices of animals for the forgiveness of sins (see Leviticus 16). They did not understand that the Lamb had been slain before the foundation of the world, nor did they know the power of the blood of Jesus.	■ **It is based on the finished work of Jesus on the cross** Jesus is the ultimate and supreme sacrifice to redeem the sin of humanity. His blood alone cleanses us once and for all (See, for example, John 19:30; Hebrews 7:27).
■ **It rejected the Messiah sent by God** That is the reason why Judaism has not had a spiritual reform, nor has it taken steps to the new. They are still waiting for the Messiah (John 1:11).	■ **It received the Messiah and King** What the nation of Israel in the first century rejected, many of the Gentiles embraced. Today all Christians—whether Gentile or Jewish in background—hear the call to take the gospel to the world, so that the entire human race receives His salvation, love and power.

■ **It had to be exercised only by males**	■ **It is exercised by men and women**
After the order of Aaron, the priesthood in the tabernacle or the temple was an office reserved exclusively for men (Leviticus 7:6).	In Jesus there is neither male nor female, slave nor free. We are all equal when it comes to entering into God's presence, presenting sacrifices, interceding, and sanctifying ourselves (See, for example, Galatians 3:26-28; Revelation 1:6).
■ **It did not have the Holy Spirit**	■ **It's under the guidance of the Holy Spirit**
The Levitical priesthood wasn't exercised under the continual inspiration and power of the Holy Spirit. They only used symbols and rituals that announced the coming of the Messiah.	The Holy Spirit lives within believers, continually guiding, empowering, helping, and counseling the Christian priesthood; in addition, the Spirit manifests the signs and wonders that happen when the gospel of the Kingdom is announced (see John 14:26).
■ **It was tribal**	■ **It is global**
In order to exercise the priesthood, a man had to have been born in the tribe of Levi (see Deuteronomy 10:8).	We are all priests. The only requirement is to have believed in Christ and to have been baptized in the Holy Spirit (1 Peter 2:9).
■ **They were only priests**	■ **We are priests and kings**
The Levitical priesthood had no governing authority; they were only priests. Hebrews 7 shows the supremacy of the priesthood of Christ over the Levitical priesthood.	The New Covenant makes us priests and kings. As priests we offer sacrifices to God. As kings we govern or rule in the Spirit, with power to bind and loose (see Matthew 16:19).

Many Christian churches avoid the Melchizedek priesthood and prefer to continue with a form of the Levitical priesthood; they follow religious rituals rather than walking in the Spirit, and they don't understand their role as priests and kings under Christ's authority. However, as we have seen, the Melchizedek priesthood nullifies not only the Levitical priesthood but also the Law (see Hebrews 7:11–19). Why is the priesthood of Christ superior to the Levitical priesthood? In Hebrews 7:20–28 we find the answer: (1) its immutability (Christ does not change) and (2) its perpetuity (He has risen and lives forever). The church of the end time is called to exercise the Melchizedek priesthood. Hence, the Bible teaches us: *"You also, as living stones, are being built up a spiritual house, a holy priesthood, to offer up spiritual sacrifices acceptable to God through Jesus Christ"* (1 Peter 2:5).

ACTIVATION

Beloved reader, if you as a Christian, have continued to exercise merely a religious priesthood, full of rites and forms, today the Holy Spirit wants to open your spiritual eyes so that you see that you need to assume the priesthood that Jesus commanded you to exercise. You are not called to say repetitive prayers; you are not called to live in condemnation, believing that your sin cannot be forgiven, and that you have to do penance or good deeds to obtain forgiveness. You are not called to minister to God without being filled with the Holy Spirit; you are not called to attend church religiously; you're not forced to read the Bible as a historical or theoretical book, much less to sing the same old songs over and over again, without revelation.

Neither are you called to think that only the pastor can be in the presence of God, or that only the pastor's prayers are answered. If you are a woman, you are not called to live as if you were a second-class citizen; Jesus died for you, too, and gave you a priesthood. As Christians we are not called to live in financial or spiritual lack, thinking that we will enjoy the Kingdom of God only after we die.

If you want to start exercising the true spiritual priesthood before God, before your family and before your church, I invite you to say the following prayer, with all your heart:

"Lord Jesus, today I pray before You, recognizing You as my High Priest. I acknowledge Your authority and power, and receive the priesthood that you exercise for me in heaven, before the Father. I ask you to forgive me for not having exercised the priesthood according to the order of Melchizedek, and I ask you to help me do so starting today. I declare that I am king and priest by the power of Your resurrection; because you opened the access, you broke down the wall that separated me from the Father, and today I can present myself before Him with spiritual sacrifices. I receive my priesthood and I commit to begin to exercise it in the manner of Christ. I declare it in Your name, beloved Jesus, amen!"

TESTIMONY

PASTOR EDGAR ORTUÑO PASTORS the largest network of churches in Bolivia, South America, with more than twenty-two thousand members in total. But it was not always like this. When he came to us, both he and his church had a great need for a true priesthood to be able to develop his ministry. He had recently graduated in Theology, and had been sent to pastor a church with a strong religious mentality; but the impartation of the priesthood of Jesus helped him to develop his own, and to establish the kingdom of God in Bolivia.

"As a Pastor in Bolivia (South America), I have seen the impartation of the priesthood through the supernatural power of God that impacted our ministry. Upon arriving at King Jesus, we were delivered of the spirit of religiosity and many mental strongholds. We started knowing God in a different way, thanks to the priesthood of our spiritual parents. The priesthood of Apostle Maldonado has taught me, has been an example for me; it has shown me that, in Christ, I can do great things, that obstacles are challenges and that

God will give me the victory through them. Prophet Ana has imparted so much in my wife that she has also gone to greater dimensions in her priesthood in the areas of intercession and deliverance. Our marriage now has a purpose and our growth does not stop. I have learned to be a son, a father and a husband, because Jesus has formed His priesthood in me. Together, my wife and I have grown in our priesthood in the ministry that is impacting different parts of South America. When we arrived at King Jesus, we were pastors of a church of about 200 members. We had started with a lot of strength, but every plan we started failed because refused to commit and we didn't know what else to do. We didn't have a spiritual covering, a priesthood that taught us, corrected us, imparted to us and guided us; that gave us spiritual fatherhood and empowered us.

"Desperate for a change, I saw Apostle Maldonado on television, and I immediately identified with his message, his personality and anointing, so I decided to attend a conference, to meet him. Once in Miami, the sermons bothered me and everything seemed strange to me. I had gone with a beggar mentality to ask for financial help and I came across something that revolutionized my spirit. I had been exercising a religious priesthood, and there I was taught to release the provision through the New Testament priesthood. God broke my beggar mentality, my religious paradigms and transformed my heart. Today we are not the same! The prophetic word received from our spiritual parents was fundamental; it gave us direction and activated us to move forward. Before we were a passive church, almost lifeless; today we are impacting our city and its surroundings. The congregation went from 200 to 4.500 people. Now we form leaders, sons and daughters of the house, to send them to raise new ministries. We see powerful miracles constantly.

"Before I couldn't mobilize my church; today, we do monthly crusades and evangelism in the streets; people get saved, they are trained and activated in leadership, the supernatural and in the purpose God gave to each one. We learned to win battles in prayer, and things happen. Our economy, which used to barely enough pay for basic utilities, has increased by 900 percent. We support an orphanage without external funding. We have radio and television programs; we built a temple for six thousand people, debt free! We established the University of the Supernatural Ministry in Bolivia to continue raising leaders, pastors, evangelists, teachers, prophets and apostles who impact the world. We supervise more than 64 churches, inside and outside of Bolivia, and we continue to grow.

"The biggest problems that we faced when we established the vision were the defamation, incomprehension and isolation of the city's pastors; but these could not prevail before the evidence of the fruits. The acceleration, breakthrough and multiplication have been supernatural! Since we received the revelation of the New Testament priesthood, everything was aligned. Everything that was impossible before, today is a reality. We advance aligned with the will of God and the power of the Holy Spirit. As kings and priests, we rule in the spiritual realm and establish the kingdom in our territory. To God be all the glory!"

3 | The New Testament Priesthood

THE PRIESTHOOD OF Jesus is superior to any other priesthood in both the Old and New Testaments. Hebrews 4:14 recognizes Christ as our *"great High Priest."* In past chapters, we have noted that Aaron was the high priest in the Levitical priesthood, but Aaron's priesthood cannot compare to that of Jesus. In fact, Jesus is the supreme example of what it means to be a priest, just as He is supreme in all things. Hebrews 7:26 says that Jesus's priesthood is *"higher than the heavens"* (Hebrew 7:26). The Scriptures affirm this truth by disclosing how *"God has highly exalted Him"* (Philippians 2:9) and how Jesus has ascended *"far above all the heavens, that He might fill all things"* (Ephesians 4:10).

Recognizing that Jesus is the perfect example of the full exercise of the priesthood, His mediation on our behalf—on the cross and with His ongoing intercession—allows us to approach God *"with confidence, so that we may receive mercy and find grace to help us in our time of need"* (Hebrews 4:16 NIV). Accordingly, any believer who desires to exercise the true and complete priesthood of Christ must fix their eyes on Him.

> *The restoration of the priesthood is linked to Jesus's second coming.*

Strengthening the Body of Christ

Today, Jesus is restoring His priesthood in the church. I believe the church, the bride, is becoming more aware of His presence because the priesthood of this generation is receiving greater heavenly authority. God is raising a new generation that is passionate about seeking His presence and about walking in the supernatural.

In the letter written to the church of Ephesus, Paul explains how Jesus gave gifts to prepare God's holy people to make the body of Christ stronger: *"He Himself gave some to be apostles, some prophets, some evangelists, and some pastors and teachers, for the equipping of the saints for the work of ministry, for the edifying of the body of Christ, till we all come to the unity of the faith and the knowledge of the Son of God, to a perfect man, to the measure of the stature of the fullness of Christ"* (Ephesians 4:11-13). The work of the ministry must continue until we are all joined together in what we believe and in what we know about the Son of God. Our goal, as a church, is to become fully grown, mature men and women – in order to resemble Christ in all His characteristics.

Characteristics of the Priesthood of Jesus

Now, let's look at what characterizes the priesthood of Jesus.

- ### Jesus Is the Revelation of the Presence of God

    Jesus was the visible expression of the presence of God here on the earth. As a priest, Jesus manifested on earth who the Father is in Heaven. He always referred to the Father as someone with whom He was very close and intimate, and He knew God's presence was always nearby. This explains why wherever He went, Jesus always changed the spiritual atmosphere and miracles happened.

    > *When the church is aware of Jesus's priesthood, it has a greater desire to be in His presence.*

    When we are aware of the purpose of Jesus's priesthood, we can understand our calling and the true power that can operate through us. The presence of God is a place where the oil of the anointing is continuous, where the breath of the Spirit blows, where we find rest, where there is fullness, peace, and enjoyment. The presence of the Almighty God is the place that the church must abide in and lead all believers into.

While living on Earth, Jesus spent hours, daily, in the presence of the Father. In one of Jesus's documented prayers, He said: *"O righteous Father! The world has not known you, but I have known you; and these have known that you sent me. And I have declared to them your name and will declare it, that the love with which you loved me may be in them, and I in them."* (John 17:25-26). In biblical language, the verb "know" doesn't only refer to mental, theoretical or superficial knowledge. For Jews, "knowing" means having an intimate experience with the person or object that is known. To be intimate with someone means to be vulnerable about the smallest details of our lives: how we think, feel, our intentions, our desires and plans, what we love and dislike, and so on. God wants us to know Him intimately.

You can have an intimate relationship with God, just as Jesus did. But you have to spend time in God's presence. You have to know Him genuinely. Once you do, you will become a carrier of His presence, and you will become protective of it. God's presence may not solve all of our problems, but, as in any intimate relationship, the most difficult issues can be resolved through communication. The presence of God always restores peace and harmony in our lives.

When the presence of God fills the air, miracles, signs, and wonders happen. The sick are healed, the oppressed are set free, and we are all empowered to live as children of God. When people receive the good news of salvation, they are reconciled with the Father, and they begin to understand what it means to be a follower of Jesus Christ.

■ Jesus Loves Prayer

Jesus dedicated the early years of His life to becoming our High Priest. He achieved this by studying the Word, offering spiritual sacrifices to God and praying for extensive hours. Jesus loved prayer because there He could spend time with the Father, connect with Him and affirm Himself in His calling. It was in the presence of God that Jesus was empowered to work miracles and challenge demonic forces. In prayer, the Holy Spirit filled Him with power, strength, wisdom, grace, and anointing to fulfill His ministry here on Earth.

Thanks to prayer, Jesus remained spiritually alert at all times. For that reason, Jesus was able to discern the time when He would be delivered to His enemies. Knowing what would happen, He prayed saying: *"O my Father, if it is possible, let this cup pass from me; nevertheless, not as I will, but as you will"* (Matthew 26:39). Jesus relied on prayer so much that He could even discern when one of His disciples was going to betray Him: "Are you still sleeping and resting? Behold, the hour is at hand, and the Son of Man is being betrayed into the hands of sinners. Rise, let us be going. See, my betrayer is at hand" (Matthew 26:45-46).

This happened the night Jesus was handed over to the Roman soldiers to be judged and crucified. He went to pray, and took with Him three of His closest disciples, but they fell asleep. In the same way today, the priesthood is asleep; that is why they don't perceive the times in which we are living. Not being prepared, they cannot warn the people or intercede before God. Nor can they discern the need to pray for those under their priesthood. This cannot go on like this! We need a spiritual awakening that leads us to watch and pray as Jesus did. In my book *Breakthrough Prayer* I teach in detail about this topic. You must read it if you wish to progress in your prayer life and be a true priest of the Highest God.

■ Jesus Is Our Intercessor

As High Priest, Jesus interceded and continues to intercede for humanity. Hence, when He knew Peter would deny Him, He mediated for him before the Father. That's why He said to Peter, *"I have prayed for you, that your faith should not fail"* (Luke 22:32). He also interceded for the unity of those who believed in Him: *"Holy Father, keep through your name those whom You have given me, that they may be one as we are. I do not pray that you should take them out of the world, but that you should keep them from the evil one. I do not pray for these alone, but also for those who will believe in me through their word"* (John 17:11, 15, 20). In essence, the whole seventeenth chapter of the gospel of John shows us how Jesus prayed for His disciples. This was born of His knowledge of God, His discernment of the times, and the exercise of His priesthood.

> *The true priest prays for more than himself, he also intercedes for others before God.*

As a priest myself, I assume the daily task of presenting my natural and spiritual families before God. In addition, I intercede for the salvation of those who don't know Christ yet. I intercede for those who are sick, those oppressed by the enemy, for those who remain enslaved to drugs and other vices, and for those who live in poverty and feel hopeless. I pray that God may free His people from all yokes of evil. If you are a man, as a priest, you also must appear before God in prayer, to pray for your children, your wife, your work, your business, your city, your nation, and the church of Jesus Christ.

■ Jesus Lived in Holiness

Jesus was the first person after the fall to live in holiness, and He modeled how to do it by sanctifying Himself for us: *"And for their sakes, I sanctify Myself, that they also may be sanctified by the truth"* (John 17:19). Every good priest must take responsibility for those whom God has placed under their priesthood, and sanctify himself for them. However, some priests of our time are irresponsible with their priesthood.

Some are more like Cain, irresponsible with their priestly duties, than like Jesus, who was fully responsible in His duties. In the Old Testament, when God asked Cain about Abel, he answered, *"I do not know. Am I my brother's keeper?"* (Genesis 4:9). However, Jesus always responds to the needs of His people with the highest expression of love: *"Greater love has no one than this than to lay down one's life for his friends"* (John 15:13).

The first sacrifice that a New Testament priest offers is their own life.

The priesthood is a call to holiness, to live apart from the world and separated for the exclusive use of God. The Scripture says: *"You are a chosen people, a royal priesthood, a holy nation, God's special possession…"* (1 Peter 2:9 NIV). This means that we were set apart for a divine purpose. We were not separated to do whatever we want, but to be priests of God living in holiness. Something is wrong when in the church the priesthood seeks to follow in the world's footsteps, compromising the truth and applying methods and forms that don't come from God. Behaving in a secular way affects our ability to reach and transform those who still don't know Jesus Christ, the Son of God.

We cannot bring holiness to a world corrupted by sin, if our priesthood is not holy.

We are living in times where there is little distinction between the behavior of those in the church and those in the world. The church has degraded all the things that are supposed to make us different. It has adapted to what people want, in the same way that financial markets adapt to what consumers demand. Church leaders have become advocates of tolerance, rather than holiness.

Today, it is frowned upon to call a sinner into repentance because it is considered offensive. The leaders who accept that view have conformed to live in deception and have perverted their priesthood, because no one can repent from a sin that they have been taught to tolerate. Even more, no one can repent from something that they don't even acknowledge as being a sin.

As I have said on previous occasions, the world has altered biblical moral values; for they are calling evil, good, and good, bad (see Isaiah 5:20). Remarkably, the church's priesthood has chosen to join with worldly corruptions, instead of standing boldly and proclaiming holiness. Peter was brave when he urged the Christians of the first century to be holy: *"But as He who called you is holy, you also be holy in all your conduct, because it is written, be holy, for I am holy"* (1 Peter 1:15-16).

There is a strong mandate from God to live in holiness and separate entirely for Him. We cannot live in the middle of two extremes. We must choose: we are cold or hot, good or bad, male or female, true or false; in other words, we must choose heaven or hell. There is nothing in between that combines the secular and the holy, that pleases God.

The purpose of holiness is to prevent mixtures.

We cannot mix with the mundane, because we will end up having a little bit of the Spirit, another part of the flesh and yet another demonic part. Just as the tree is known for its fruit, but the essence of its life is in its root; human fruits come from what is in the heart of man. This conditions the intentions and motives that lead us to act. When what we do comes from the Spirit, but the motivation is from the flesh; a mixture is produced that profanes holiness. However, it is common to see priests mixing the things of the Spirit with demonic ones; connecting a little bit of the gift with a lot from the flesh. This hurts those around them and ends up destroying what they have built.

Later we will address the subject of holiness in greater detail; because, praying for the people, God put a burden in my spirit for the holiness of the priesthood. And I feel that, as a priest, I must warn, exhort and make a call for holiness today. Are you willing to respond to that call? My prayer is that you are.

■ Jesus Came to Serve

Today, many leaders in the church have become authoritarian over their congregations. They don't serve their people, but they expect to be served. They see the priesthood as a profession. They subjugate their people and feel superior to them. That is not the true priesthood; Christ always served others before Himself. Jesus taught His disciples the difference between exercising authority and serving: *"The rulers of the Gentiles lord it over them, and those who are great exercise authority over them."* But, He also told them that in the Kingdom it should not be like that, because *"the Son of Man did not come to be served, but to serve, and to give His life a ransom for many"* (Matthew 20:25, 28). Jesus, as High Priest didn't come to overpower anyone, but to serve everyone, giving Himself entirely for our salvation.

A priest places his life at the service of his family and others that God has placed under his authority.

■ Jesus Loves His Church and Always Takes Care of It.

Many men do not know their true role; and for that reason, they mistreat and subdue their family. Such men demand a lot from their wife and children, even though they don't fulfill their priestly commitment. The true priest loves and cares for his wife and children, giving up his own life for them, just as Jesus did. Paul wrote to the men of Ephesus, explaining their roles as priests: *"Husbands, love your wives, just as Christ also loved the church and gave Himself for her, that He might sanctify and cleanse her... So husbands ought to love their own wives as their own bodies; he who loves his wife loves himself"* (Ephesians 5:25-26, 28).

> *The true priest loves his wife and protects his children, guiding them in the ways of the Lord and giving himself for them.*

■ Jesus Offered Himself as a Sacrifice

In the Old Testament, high priests had to offer animal sacrifices for the sins of the people continually, *"but when this priest had offered for all time one sacrifice for sins, he sat down at the right hand of God, for by one sacrifice he has made perfect forever those who are being made holy"* (Hebrews 10:12, 14 NIV). Today, it is no longer necessary to sacrifice animals. Every priest must follow the example of Jesus Christ in offering spiritual sacrifices instead. Peter taught this concept well: *"You also, as living stones, are being built up a spiritual house, a holy priesthood, to offer up spiritual sacrifices acceptable to God through Jesus Christ"* (1 Peter 2:5).

With this we understand that, while animal sacrifices aren't offered anymore for the forgiveness of sins, the priest must still *"...continually offer to God a sacrifice of praise—the fruit of lips that openly profess his name"* (Hebrews 13:15 NIV). The sacrificing of animals ended when Jesus made the ultimate sacrifice, dying for our sins. However, God the Father still receives the living, spiritual sacrifices of His priests, which we present and surrender to Him in love, holiness, and service on behalf of our families and our congregations. Having revelation of this, in his letter to the Romans, Paul wrote: *"I beseech you therefore, brethren...that you present your bodies a living sacrifice, holy, acceptable to God..."* (Romans 12:1).

> *Every priest must offer spiritual sacrifices of praise, personal surrender and holiness.*

■ Jesus Has Power and Authority

We need to learn from Jesus, who after overcoming the temptation in the desert, *"returned in the power of the Spirit to Galilee"* (Luke

4:14) to undo the works of the devil. Today, priests do not know how to exercise power and authority in the face of sickness, financial crisis, divorce, their children's rebellion, fear, insecurity, crime, drug addiction, spiritual oppression, sin, injustice, and so forth.

By His intimate relationship with the heavenly Father and through prayer, Jesus received revelation that He was Christ, the Anointed, King, and Priest on Earth. However, to experience that revelation, He had to pay for the rescue of the human race; and the price was His blood. Everything described above gave Jesus the right to exercise, as a man, the power and the authority of God. That's why people marveled when Jesus practiced His righteous authority, *"...and spoke among themselves, saying, 'What a word this is! For with authority and power, He commands the unclean spirits, and they come out'"* (Luke 4:36).

On another occasion, Jesus's disciples, who still didn't fully understand His identity and authority, asked themselves, *"Who is this? He commands even the winds and the water, and they obey him"* (Luke 8:25). Some of the same people who questioned Jesus' authority also wanted His power: *"The whole multitude sought to touch Him, for power went out from Him and healed them all"* (Luke 6:19). Jesus exercised power and authority because He did the will of the Father. Priests today can walk in that same power, because Jesus gave it to us and we can use it in His name.

> **When we exercise the priesthood in the same way Jesus did, His power will manifest in and through us.**

■ Jesus is the Head of the Church

Many think that being a head is giving orders or forcing others to do their will above all else. In reality, that is authoritarianism; and it is not politics of the Kingdom of God. Jesus was placed as the Head of the church because He gave Himself completely for her; because He loves her, sanctifies her, cares for her, protects her, takes her to know the Father, and will soon return for her. We as believers know that, in Christ we have salvation, deliverance, healing, prosperity, love, forgiveness, and strength. We know that God does not change, that His word remains forever, and that He is our advocate, not a judge. Christ is who represents us before the Father. His love is unconditional, and He is the sincerest example of what it means to be a head.

If husbands can recognize that Christ is the head of the church, then they will identify their role as a head to their family: *"The husband is head of the wife, as also Christ is head of the church, and He is the Savior of the body"* (Ephesians 5:23). Today's priests must learn to be the head of their families and the church, according to the model of the priesthood of Jesus. As Jesus submits to the Father, men must submit to Christ, so that their wives and children may submit to them. It is a leadership founded on love and service.

As head of the family, the man is called to present spiritual sacrifices to God on behalf of his wife and children.

ACTIVATION

As you continue reading this book, you will note that I intend to impart to you a sense of urgency to acknowledge a holy priesthood. I want you to feel the demand from God to restore the priesthood to be like the one that Jesus modeled for us. Jesus accepted His mission of coming to earth as a man, and stripped Himself of His divine attributes to fulfill His purpose. He showed that it is possible to sanctify ourselves, to dedicate ourselves to prayer, to love our family and give ourselves to them in service. It is also possible to intercede and exercise the power and authority of God here on earth. We must present ourselves as a living sacrifice before the Father, just as Jesus did. Today, if you feel as though you have not been living the priesthood Jesus has modeled for you, then this call is for you. Please pray the following prayer with me.

> *"Lord Jesus, today I decided to answer to Your calling and to surrender to my personal requests. I want to be a priest that follows in Your footsteps and models after You in every action. Today, I make the decision to dedicate more of myself to You. I make the decision to spend more time in Your presence and in prayer. I want to know You more and become a carrier of Your presence. I commit to learning how to love my wife and children Your way and to give myself in service to them. I want to be that husband, that father, that loves and cares for his family like you love and take care of the church. I will want to be the head Your way; interceding before God for my family and representing them before the Father. Above all, I commit to living a life of holiness, getting away from sin, and from everything that prevents me from being the priest that You want to raise in me. By Your grace and Your strength, I will be a priest of the New Testament with power and authority to destroy the works of the enemy. I pray in the mighty name of Jesus. Amen!*

TESTIMONIES

Next, I will share a series of testimonies about what the restoration of the priesthood can do in a home, in children, and in the church. What you will read here can happen to you if you decide to exercise priesthood just as Jesus modeled it. Your testimony could be the next restoration of priesthood!

LILIANA WAS AN ATHEIST; she was introduced to in our ministry about the same time her marriage was on the verge of ending. As you will soon find out, the love of the Father restored her and her marriage. This is her testimony:

"My life was a complete mess until I came to King Jesus Ministries and had an experience with God. I use to have a very toxic relationship with my husband; so much so that I used to tell him that only a miracle from God would help us fall back in love. However, since I was an atheist, I was confident that would never happen. Soon after, my husband and I divorced, but we had shared custody of our son. My husband and son's relationship was drifting apart, and I felt the burden of divorce harmfully affecting my life and my son's.

"One day my friend from Spain was visiting Miami and insisted on visiting King Jesus Ministries. I decided to stay with her and listen in on the sermon Apostle Maldonado was preaching. To this day, I feel as though that sermon was specifically for me, even though I was in a crowd of thousands of people. When I heard Apostle Maldonado speak, my life started changing completely. As a spoke about priesthood and its roles, I knew I didn't want my son to grow up without his father: his head and his priest.

"I still believed I would never reconcile with my husband, but as a priest myself, I knew what was right for my family. I decided to invite my, now, ex-husband to the church's deliverance retreat. While they were ministering to him, I asked God to deliver him and change him. But, to my surprise, God also delivered me and changed me. That day, I was delivered from years of forgiveness that I held against my husband. I was finally able to forgive him, and we are a family again. Christ restored our marriage. Today, my son is growing up with both his parents living at home. Together, as a family, we serve in the church and host a House of Peace . Nowadays, we get to testify that Jesus is alive and that He is the High Priest that changed and delivered us. His presence has brought love, an abundance of peace and multiplication to our lives. We are currently expecting a second child, and we are thrilled! Glory to God!"

LAUDY, AT AGE 15, felt lost in the direction of her life after her father abandoned her and her family. It wasn't until the priesthood of Christ came and restored her entirely that she felt whole again. This is her testimony:

"When I was fifteen years old, my dad abandoned my family and I, so I didn't know what it was to have a father figure at home. After that day, I held so much resentment and bitterness in my heart that I looked for refuge in drugs, and I fell into all other sorts of sins. As a result of my rebellious uprising, I became pregnant. I knew I didn't want to raise a child without a father so I decided to have an abortion. The abortion brought a substantial amount of shame and guilt into my life. I knew it was time for a change. I decided to go back to God and reconcile with Him. That day changed my life forever. I have never experienced the love of a father as I did in God's presence. All my emptiness disappeared, layer after layer. I knew God's love removed it. For the first time, ever, I understood what a true example of Jesus's priesthood was like. After ten years of not speaking to my natural father, today I have a healthy relationship with him. Now, we pray together as a family, fulfilling the original plan of God. Jesus transformed my life and my relationships! He has changed my way of looking at priesthood and helped me develop a loving relationship with my natural father. All the glory goes to God because His love transformed my life!"

DIEGO, A PASTOR IN Argentina, tells us of his testimony of how he encountered true priesthood through our ministry. His church has now expanded and is educating other young priests. This is his testimony:

"I have watched Apostle Maldonado's sermons for many years from Argentina, South America, through the internet. I had always dreamt of going to the United States to meet him and have an encounter with the power of God through his ministry. When God made my dream a reality, I started to experience a change in me as a priest, both in my family and in our church. To take on the priesthood of Jesus was not easy. I had to learn to love, sacrifice, and pray differently from before. However, God was very faithful to me throughout this process. The teachings of Apostle Maldonado were the guidance that I needed to raise priesthood in our house and in my church. Our ministry rapidly began to walk under open Heavens with power and authority.

We have seen the love and priesthood of God in so many areas of our life, especially our finances. By God's grace, we were able to buy a new building with a capacity to fit our growing congregation of 2,500 people. In this new building, we have been able to disciple leaders who advance the kingdom of God. Apostle Maldonado's priestly teachings and examples have led us to actively and passionately follow Jesus's priesthood. Every time we attend King Jesus Ministry's conferences and events, we experience something new from Christ and His priesthood. We have come to know God more as a Father and a healer than ever before. Today I am happy to know that I am prepared as a priest, and a leader, of the people He has trusted me with. God is good, Amen!"

4 | Responsibilities of the Priest

ON THE SEVENTH month of every year, the Hebrew people of the Old Testament used to gather together in holy convocation to offer burnt offerings to God for the forgiveness of their sins (see Numbers 29:11). The priest played a fundamental role in this ceremony since he was the one who presented the sacrifices to the Lord. The sacrifices consisted of killing one goat for each person who wanted their sins and faults of the past year to be removed. After the new covenant was established in Jesus Christ, it was no longer necessary to sacrifice animals, because the sacrifice of our High Priest, the holy Lamb, Jesus Christ, was made once and *"for all time"* (see Hebrews 10:12). Jesus redeemed us with His blood. This means that He paid the redemption price to free us from bondage, and His sacrifice was greater than all the animal sacrifices of the Old Testament.

In this chapter, I want to introduce to you the essential responsibilities of the New Testament priesthood. As we have learned in previous chapters, a priest is someone who offers spiritual sacrifices to God and is himself a *"living sacrifice"* (Romans 12:1): *"For every high priest taken from among men is appointed for men in things pertaining to God, that he may offer both gifts and sacrifices for sins"* (Hebrews 5:1). The primary responsibilities of a holy priesthood are to offer spiritual sacrifices, carry the presence of God, teach the Scriptures, lead and guide, be a prophetic voice of the sound of God, and rule in the Spirit through prayer. Let's look at each of these responsibilities in more depth.

1. To Offer Spiritual Sacrifices Before God

By His death and resurrection, Jesus gave us access to the Father, to present spiritual sacrifices to God through our great High Priest. The Bible calls us to build our spiritual house and to learn to offer spiritual sacrifices: *"You also, as living stones, are being built up a spiritual house, a holy priesthood, to offer up spiritual sacrifices acceptable to God through Jesus Christ"* (1 Peter 2:5).

What is a spiritual sacrifice?

Defined in the most straightforward way, a spiritual sacrifice is everything and anything that can be offered to God that brings us closer to Him. The most common spiritual sacrifices are prayer, worship, fasting, righteous acts, offerings of money, and the giving of our time. Spiritual sacrifices are like a set of tools that Jesus left behind for us so that, as the Holy Spirit guides us, we can grow in our relationship with Him, carry His presence, know His will, and empower ourselves to fulfill His purpose for us here on earth. Can someone be a priest without praying? Absolutely not. A priest who does not pray, worship, or offer other spiritual sacrifices is forfeiting his place in the kingdom of God. We must die to the desires of our flesh and to the vanity of the world. The priest must strive to be a living sacrifice for God.

> *A church will never grow above the level of its priesthood.*

The level of priestly exercise will determine the level of power in a church. This means that if men don't perform their priestly tasks, there will be no spiritual activity in either their homes or their churches. If men fail to function as priests, their connection with God will be weakened, and His life will not flow accordingly. It is necessary to make urgent changes if you're not fulfilling your priestly functions. Otherwise, your life, your family, and your church may become stagnant. For instance, many times, parents have approached me about concerns over their rebellious child. Their child may be lost in drugs, alcohol, even crime, but what the parents do not understand is that the root of their child's misbehavior is often their own failure to exercise the priesthood at home.

The main function of a New Testament priest is to offer sacrifices, prayer, and worship.

2. To Carry the Presence of God

As described earlier, the Melchizedek priesthood foreshadowed the priesthood of the New Testament. Before the Hebrew people settled into the Promised Land, the sanctuary of God's presence (the ark of the covenant) had to be moved every time the people moved. This task was only allowed to be done by the priests. (See, for example, Joshua 3:17.) Today, we do not need to have a physical sanctuary, for the priestly function can reach its fullness when each priest becomes a carrier of the presence of God.

What must a New Testament priest do to carry the presence of God? First, a priest accesses the presence of God through a continuous life of prayer and worship, which produces an intimate relationship with Him. Eventually, the priest becomes one with God in heart and mind. This leads the priest to live a life of holiness and avoid mixing the things of the flesh with the things of the Spirit.

A carrier of the presence of God automatically carries a spiritual legacy; their voice is anointed, and the mercy of God follows them (see Exodus 33:18-19). The enemy hates it when you, as a priest, pray and worship, because then you become an agent of change in the kingdom of God.

Prayer forms the presence of God in you, while intimacy with God helps you carry that presence daily.

Peter is an excellent example of a carrier of God's presence. He was recognized for carrying the presence of the Lord wherever He went. He was so filled with the presence that those who needed healing followed him just so that the presence might fall on them: *"They brought the sick out into the streets and laid them on beds and couches, that at least the shadow of Peter passing by might fall on some of them. Also a multitude gathered from the surrounding cities to Jerusalem, bringing sick people and those who were tormented by unclean spirits, and they were all healed"* (Acts 5:15-16). Peter is not an exception to carrying the presence of God—he is the rule. You and I can carry the presence of God just like Peter did because the same Holy Spirit—the same presence of God—who rested on Peter is available to all who seek Him wholeheartedly.

If you know you have been called to one of the offices of the fivefold ministry—apostle, prophet, pastor, evangelist or teacher—your prayer life and sacrifice must be an example to your church or ministry. If you are not a carrier of God's presence, then you won't be able to properly exercise the ministry you have been called to. You will also have trouble leading others to know Christ and experience His love and power.

3. To Teach the Scriptures

Teaching the Scriptures is not an assignment only for the fivefold ministry—we are *all* called to teach others about Jesus Christ (1 Peter 2:9) and the truths and principles of God's Word. We must be careful not to produce a generation that is ignorant of the Scriptures. Believers are responsible for learning more about God and His Word, while also teaching others what they have learned. God doesn't want us to reject His knowledge; He wants us to live by His Word: *"Because you have rejected knowledge, I also will reject you from being priest for Me; because you have forgotten the law of your God, I also will forget your children"* (Hosea 4:6). As priests, we should be able to teach God's Word to those under our authority.

Josiah, the Bible tells us, was the last virtuous king of Israel. He began to reign when he was only eight years old. At age twelve, while his people cleansed Judah and Jerusalem from the Asherah images (to the false goddess) and demolished the altars of the Baals (false gods), among the debris, they found the book of Jehovah's law. This was the law that was given originally by God to Moses. The young king commanded Israel to follow the laws given to Moses. He made sure the temple and the priesthood were sanctified, and he restored the teaching of Scripture to the nation. He decreed that the Levites should teach the Scriptures to the people. (See, for example, 2 Chronicles 34:14; 35:3.)

Josiah himself also read and taught the Scriptures to his people. He made sure Judah did not depart from the law of the Lord all the days of his reign. *"For the lips of a priest should keep knowledge, and people should seek the law from his mouth; for he is the messenger of the Lord of hosts"* (Malachi 2:7).

4. To Lead and Guide

There are significant differences between leading and guiding people. When a priest leads, he points the way, and he goes ahead of the people. When he guides, he gives advice and instructions on what to do and where to go. To be an effective priest, you must know how to combine leadership with spiritual guidance. For a priest to guide and lead effectively, he must first be led and guided by the Holy Spirit. *"For as many as are led by the Spirit of God, these are sons of God"* (Romans 8:14). Discerning the guidance of the Holy Spirit is one of the marks of a mature son of God. A mature son is someone who is competent in exercising the priesthood to which he has been called.

> **Every leader must set an example of being the first to submit to the commandments set by God.**

The purpose of setting a priestly example is so that people may be influenced to live a priestly lifestyle as well. A priest is known for how well he leads those under him, both in his family and in the church. People will imitate what they see their priest doing. Paul encouraged us to imitate our priestly leaders: *"Imitate me, just as I also imitate Christ"* (1 Corinthians 11:1).

Here the term "imitate" doesn't mean to be a copy, but rather a replica. What is the difference? When we "copy" someone else's life, we are essentially plagiarizing them—presenting that other person's work as our own. But when we replicate or reproduce someone else's life, it is because we have received the revelation of the principles they taught or demonstrated to us, and we repeat them.

What I am teaching here is not theory for me; I practice it daily. I imitate what my spiritual covering does, and the people under my authority do the same, because when someone has the revelation of the importance of priesthood, a natural consequence is that they can easily submit to authority.

5. To Be a Prophetic Voice of the Sound of God

The root of worship is prophetic and it carries revelation.

The priesthood carries the sound of worship to God. When David brought the ark of God's presence to Jerusalem (the second time), he put the Levites in charge of this task: *"David spoke to the leaders of the Levites to appoint their brethren to be the singers accompanied by instruments of music, stringed instruments, harps, and cymbals, by raising the voice with resounding joy. Chenaniah, leader of the Levites, was instructor in charge of the music, because he was skillful"* (1 Chronicles 15:16, 22).

This was also the case when David organized the ministers who would serve in the temple that Solomon would build. From the tribe of Levi, he separated *"four thousand were gatekeepers, and four thousand praised the Lord with musical instruments, 'which*

I made,' said David, 'for giving praise'" (1 Chronicles 23:5). *"Moreover, David and the captains of the army separated for the service some of the sons of Asaph, of Heman, and of Jeduthun, who should prophesy with harps, stringed instruments, and cymbals... [The latter] prophesied with a harp to give thanks and to praise the Lord"* (1 Chronicles 25:1, 3).

A priest must set himself apart to worship God.

Through David we understand that musicians are also priests and that their function is to prophesy, worship, and praise God with their instruments.

The priesthood of a musician consists of knowing God, playing well, and dedicating themselves and their talents to God -in prayer and the knowledge of Scripture-, to prophesy with their voices and instruments. Many worshipers need this revelation because, even though they know their calling, they don't know how to exercise their priesthood in worship. If sanctification is demanded of every priest, the demand upon the praise and worship ministers is even greater. Musicians need to have a pure heart towards God, only this way He will pour out His glory through them in worship.

What kind of musicians are standing at the altar in our churches? Today, it seems like the only requirement for playing an instrument or leading worship is to have musical talent. For the most part, the musicians who are in a position of priesthood have a weak, unsteady prayer life, or they simply don't have it; they don't know the Scriptures, and have no idea of their spiritual responsibilities or the divine demand to be a holy priesthood. That is the reason why there is no presence of God in some churches. There is a sound, but there are also mixtures of the Spirit and the flesh, and God's presence cannot manifest there.

Without the prophetic guidance of the Holy Spirit, worship will not carry the sound of heaven.

In our ministry, our singers and musicians are trained and edified in their spiritual priesthood to stand at the altar with a full understanding of their spiritual roles and responsibilities. For example, each time praise leaders are going to lead praise and worship in service, they set aside the day before to fast, pray, and seek the revelation of what God will do. So, when they go up to the altar, they are carrying the presence of God and can release new and prophetic songs that bring the sound of heaven to our services. This explains why, when we make the call of salvation, many people accept Jesus, and when we minister miracles, many people are healed. The supernatural atmosphere of God's power, love, and grace was created during the praise and worship.

The Commercialization of Worship

A few months ago, I was teaching a series to my church called "The Power of Speaking in Spiritual Tongues." During my preaching, I asked one of our saxophonists to play. Before he began to play, he first prayed in tongues; then, with his instrument, he unleashed the sound he felt from heaven. The presence of God immediately fell. It was indescribable! Everyone in the service felt it; even those who follow us online in other continents were impacted by the presence of God that manifested through that priest musician. That can only occur when a musician lives consecrated to God and has the revelation of his priestly function in worship.

The presence of God is missing from much of the church because worship has been commercialized.

When we commercialize worship, the supernatural "substance" in it dissipates. The songs become egocentric and self-seeking, relating more to need, flesh, and emotions. They are not from God or for God, but to become famous and sell. These songs don't carry the glory or presence of God, and most of them sound like a list of personal requests: "Lord, bless me, touch me, give me, heal me." We need more songs that exalt the glory of God, the blood of Christ, the power of His name, the finished work of the cross, the faithfulness of God's Word, the guidance of the Holy Spirit, and God's great works, virtues, glory, and majesty.

The Corruption of Worship

When we worship without righteousness in our hearts, we offer "strange fire" to God.

When the priesthood that must carry the sound of worship to God is not righteous in their hearts, the only thing they can offer is *"strange fire"* (Leviticus 10:1 KJV), and God rejects strange fire. Strange worship can seem godly, use the right words, sounds, and even the right voice, but it does not have God's presence since it comes from the flesh and it only feeds the flesh. In many churches, worship is contaminated because the priesthood is contaminated. Anyone can be at the altar and pray, sing, or play an instrument. Furthermore, some churches allow at their altar people who haven't given their life to Christ. They hire musicians who are not Christian or who don't belong to their congregations. Some of those people may play in bars, watch pornography, or practice witchcraft, and the next day, they are playing at church. In these cases, the altar is stained, and that is the reason why the presence of God is not there.

Worship reveals the spiritual activity of the heart.

If there is iniquity in the heart of the priest-musicians, they will release this into the atmosphere through their voice or instrument, and contaminate it. A corrupt heart projects corruption into their atmosphere because it lives apart from the holiness of God. This was Lucifer's sin. He ministered worship in heaven and was cast out because iniquity and moral perversion were found in his heart; he had mixtures: *"You were perfect in your ways from the day you were created, till iniquity was found in you"* (Ezekiel 28:15).

Before we assign musicians and singers to serve at the altar, we must ask ourselves, "Have these musicians sacrificed something for God?" If they genuinely are priests of God, they will bring His presence. That is the test! Many times, we have to confront those who are not aligned with the commands and will of God, so that they may be sanctified and restored. But, if they don't repent, don't sanctify themselves, and don't dedicate themselves to the Word and prayer, we must, appropriately, replace them.

6. Rule in the Spirit Through Prayer

> **The priest offers sacrifices to God, but the king governs on God's behalf.**

God is calling His people to exercise the same priesthood that Jesus did, in the *"order of Melchizedek"* (Psalm 110:4). As priests, we must carry the presence of God, teach the Word, and lead and guide the people. We must also be the prophetic voice that brings the sound of God to earth. In his home, the man is king, and a king must govern. A king has the authority to establish laws and to decree through faith and prayer. A man who is king has received authorization from God to set rules, as long as he is subject to Christ. The Bible shows us a gallery of heroes of the faith, men and women who exercised such righteous government in the Spirit, *"who through faith subdued kingdoms, worked righteousness, obtained promises, stopped the mouths of lions"* (Hebrews 11:33).

Ruling in the Spirit

When Christ ascended, He left us as His legal representatives on earth, and these are the areas over which we must exercise spiritual authority:

- Our own spirit (Proverbs 15:12)
- Our home (1 Timothy 3:4)
- The house of God (2 Timothy 3:4-5)
- People who don't submit to authority.
- The enemy and his works (1 John 3:8)

The apostolic ministry of the New Testament is equivalent to the kingship of the Old Testament. That's why God has appointed certain leaders in the church: *"God has appointed these in the church: first apostles, second prophets, third teachers, after that miracles, then gifts of healings, helps, administrations, varieties of tongues"* (1 Corinthians 12:28).

The weight of God's governance is higher on the apostles and prophets.

I can personally say that, when the authority as a priest and a king comes over me to decree onto nations, governments, and even in nature, amazing occurrences happen. The same can happen to you when you operate under God's authority. Therefore, if you are an apostle, you cannot mix the things of the flesh with the things of the Spirit. As a governing apostle, you cannot do business with, or be a part of, the activities of any government that corrupts the commandments of God. You must stay on the sidelines and pray for God to take control. Only those who rule from the Spirit realm will be the voice of God that warns about the times to come, in order to lead people to repentance. The rulers of those governments may eventually need your advice, but they will not be able to use you or use the church of Christ as part of their political strategies and hidden agendas.

The apostles of the third day—of the resurrected Christ—are people capable of decreeing God's wrath or God's favor over a city.

Adam was the first person to whom God gave dominion over the earth. In doing so, the Lord introduced two words to us: rule and subdue: *"Then God said, let us make man in our image, according to our likeness; let them have dominion over the fish of the sea, over the birds of the air, and over the cattle, over all the earth and over every creeping thing that creeps on the earth [...] Then God blessed them, and God said to them, Be fruitful and multiply; fill the earth and subdue it; have dominion over the fish of the sea, over the birds of the air, and over every living thing that moves on the earth"* (Genesis 1:26, 28).

God gave Adam power and authority to subdue and subjugate everything He had created. This means: to put under our feet, to take by force and to dominate. But when the serpent entered the Garden of Eden, Adam didn't do what he should have done. He was supposed to lead his wife and subdue the serpent; but he didn't.

The word *subdue* is a military term that implies exercising force. We can subjugate the earth and the animals, but not other people. We must lead or govern people with wisdom. We can lead those who submit to authority; but it is necessary to govern when someone doesn't submit to it.

God never wanted us to force rules onto people because it contradicts the principle of the priesthood and free will. Jesus didn't govern His disciples; He led them by example and with wisdom. *"But Jesus called them to Himself and said, you know that the rulers of the Gentiles lord it over them, and those who are great exercise authority over them. Yet it shall not be so among you; but whoever desires to become great among you, let him be your servant. And whoever desires to be first among you, let him be your slave"* (Matthew 20:25-27). A leader without God will always subjugate and try to control. Coincidently, people without God cannot be led because they do not naturally submit to authority.

How to Rule in the Spirit Through Prayer

Only if the church prays and exercises its priesthood effectively will the ungodly laws of a country change.

Prayer is the place where God can change ungodly laws and nullify governmental decrees and judicial decisions that are contrary to His Word. Divine justice will always be above any human law. For example, by praying, believers can supernaturally receive immigration documents that have been delayed or get back a house that was to be auctioned off. They can see the return of goods that were stolen, or have a court sentence be reduced or dismissed altogether. They can witness the release of an evangelist imprisoned in a country where it is forbidden to preach the gospel. These types of things can happen when we are under God's superior government.

Prayer is the place where the laws of nature can be interrupted.

In the book of Daniel, we find how the laws of nature were interrupted when Daniel prayed and the lions in the den did not attack him: *"...So the king gave the command, and they brought Daniel and cast him into the den of lions [...] And when he came to the den, he cried out with a lamenting voice to Daniel. The king spoke, saying to Daniel, Daniel, servant of the living God, has your God, whom you serve continually, been able to deliver you from the lions? Then Daniel said to the king, "O king, live forever! My God sent His angel and shut the lions' mouths, so that they have not hurt me, because I was found innocent before Him; and also, O king, I have done no wrong before you"* (Daniel 6:16, 20-22). Thanks to Daniel's prayer life, God overrode the natural order; the lions that would have devoured the prophet Daniel didn't even touch him.

You have the power and authority to bind and loosen, to prohibit and permit, to declare illegal or legal, illegitimate or legitimate anything on earth in the name of Jesus. With this I tell you that we have the power to declare our own God-given destiny. Neither the devil, nor man, nor circumstances, nor anything else can stop that destiny. Jesus gave us the keys of the kingdom of heaven: *"And I will give you the keys of the kingdom of heaven, and whatever you bind on earth will be bound in heaven, and whatever you loose on earth will be loosed in heaven"* (Matthew 16:19).

> **Everything we declare legal on earth,
> God will declare legal in heaven.**

I challenge all priests to begin to make spiritual warfare through prayer, from a position of kingship. We are living in intense days on earth. Nature is in turmoil, wars are ongoing, diseases and illnesses are spreading, sin and iniquity are becoming ever so common even in the church. These intense days require priests and kings to take greater authority over all these situations. What will you do? Will you rise in prayer, or will you remain spiritually asleep? Pray until something breaks in the spiritual world! Only then will you be able to see it manifest in the natural realm.

What legitimizes the priesthood is their prayer life. If Jesus said that His house would be called *"a house of prayer"* (Matthew 21:13), it cannot be that the priesthood doesn't pray. We must be kings and priests (see, for example, Revelation 1:6) who constantly live in prayer. We must understand that one of our main responsibilities is to pray. The Lord wants to give us a new level of authority, but that implies that the priesthood must be restored, resuming a life of prayer.

> **Jesus made us kings and priests to exercise dominion,
> power, and authority over every work of the enemy.**

As priests, we must be prepared to wage war against all demonic power. We need to learn to rule with power and authority in every situation. As priests of the kingdom, God has given us access to riches, miracles, provision, houses, land, and other properties, but we must go and take them by spiritual force. We must destroy the enemy's plans and nullify his strategies. We can achieve breakthroughs in all areas if we learn to pray and rule with the authority God gave us.

ACTIVATION

As we move forward with the revelation of the responsibilities of a New Testament priest, the demand of the Holy Spirit on you, as a reader, also increases. I believe that you cannot have reached this point without feeling the challenge of making a decision to change and assume your priestly functions. If you feel as though your priesthood hasn't been as effective as you would like, then raise your standards and start offering spiritual sacrifices to God. If you were asleep, it is time to start praying and seeking the presence of the Father; if you were bound by ignorance, the challenge is to set yourself free from it. Ask for forgiveness and turn away from everything that goes against your sanctification and dedication to the priesthood. This will, in turn, bring the blessings that your family and congregation have lacked.

If you want to bring God's presence to your home or ministry, pray this prayer aloud:

> *"Lord Jesus, I thank You for bringing this revelation into my life. Thank You because, despite my foolishness and ignorance, You have interceded for me before the Father so that I will not be left without the revelation of the priesthood that You have delegated to me. Thank You for bringing the knowledge of the responsibilities that are needed to be activated to practice a holy priesthood. I ask You for forgiveness for not having been exercising my priesthood at home or in my ministry; forgive me for my lack of fear, diligence, obedience, and knowledge. Remove from me everything that prevents me from devoting myself to the priesthood. Give me Your power to overcome, and Your grace to do Your perfect will. I want to become a carrier*

of Your presence in my home, and wherever I go, so I can manifest Your presence. I want to offer spiritual sacrifices daily to be able to grow closer to You. I want to praise You, worship You, offer prayer, and to fast in a consistent manner. I want to offer You my time, service, acts of justice, money, and death to self so that You can live in me and through me; to fulfill Your will above mine. I want to learn and be trained to be able to teach the Scriptures to my children and to those You bring under my leadership. Give me a passion for Your word! Engrave Your word in my heart so that I can live in it, and so that I may impart it to others as a living word. I want to learn to be the leader and to guide my family. I want to lead them to Your path and will. In crisis situations, show me the way so that I can show it to my family and my ministry. I want to be a prophetic voice of what You are saying. Give me the grace to worship You in spirit and truth; to bring Your presence to more people so that more people can be saved, healed, delivered, and empowered by Your Holy Spirit. I want to learn to govern in the spiritual world through prayer. I want to be like You; who lived in obedience to the Father and therefore, when He spoke, even nature obeyed; who inspired His disciples and empowered them to establish Your Kingdom on Earth. Teach me, Lord, to exercise the responsibilities of priesthood! I pray all this in Your name, Jesus. Amen!"

TESTIMONIES

PASTOR TOMMY AND SARAHI Acosta pastor one of our daughter churches in the city of Fort Lauderdale, Florida. During one of their services, a young girl with an incurable disease was brought by her parents who testified of the power of declaring healing with priestly authority. This is their testimony:

"A three-year-old girl was brought by her parents to our church. She had been diagnosed with Pityriasis rubra pilaris, a rare disease that left her without eyebrows or eyelashes and caused her skin to peel off and constantly bleed. In Peru, her country of origin, she had been examined by many doctors, but they all agreed it had no cure, and that she should remain under a prescribed treatment for the rest of her life. Desperate to give her daughter a normal life, the mother traveled to the United States, seeking help. Here they went to many places, but the answer was the same: there was no definitive cure. Furthermore, the medicine was incredibly expensive; a cost the family could not afford. Desperate for help, they came to our church, King Jesus Ministries in Broward, where we started praying for their daughter. We taught her parents how to pray and decree with priestly authority health upon their daughter's life. Little by little, prayer after prayer, her skin started being restored, and she was able to stop taking her medications. Her eyebrows and eyelashes started growing back and finally, all of her skin was completely healed as if she had never been sick. Today, the girl has a normal life. She is a living testimony of the power of prayer, and that Christ is alive and full of power!"

BELÉN LOSA IS CONSIDERED a psalmist in our music ministry and carries a prophetic voice. She exercises the spiritual priesthood worshipping on the altar, both in our church and in the nations.

"I give thanks to God for my spiritual father for how he has instructed, and guided us, musicians, to go into deeper levels of worship. He has taught us many lessons, such as: how to build an atmosphere from which God wants to speak, how to carry the prophetic "burden" in worship, how to become aware of the priesthood in worship, and how to exercise it. Apostle's teachings have led me to see notorious and effective results in priesthood worship.

"When I understood that the priest was the one who took the initiative to offer sacrifices to God for them self, and for the people, the fear of God came over me, and I felt the responsibility of preparing myself to be that pure outlet that God can use to lead others to His presence. I also have come to learn that a priest in music must exercise their priesthood as a king; we must declare what we hear in the spirit. Every time I have to lead praise and worship I feel a prophetic "burden" come upon me. If I know I will be leading, then I start preparing myself at the beginning of the week: I start preparing in prayer and worship, and reading the word of God. When I prepare this way, it is easier to see, hear, and perceive the Spirit. Then, when we sing and play on the altar, the spirit of God provokes changes in the atmosphere and the people. The sounds released on the alter have the life of God and produce powerful movements in the spiritual realm.

"The same powerful sounds are also produced when we accompany the Apostle on his travels. I have been in many different environments and atmospheres. Depending on the country, there may be atmospheres of unbelief, spiritual hardness, and witchcraft; all of them very strong. But, can only be broken with prophetic worship. Every time we go to a different country to minister next to our spiritual father, we take the prophetic "burden," and we seek God as a team. We are one in prayer, intercession, and worship. Thanks to this unity, we have seen an infinite number of miracles, salvations, deliverances, and lives transformed by the power of God".

MY TESTIMONIES

Ruling Over Nature:

In September 2017, Hurricane Irma was approaching the coasts of Florida with a category five strength, the highest level of destruction that hurricane winds produce. Its maximum winds were 185 mph –almost 300 kph– when it was quickly approaching Miami. It came to be considered the most powerful storm in the Atlantic Ocean that Fall. Hurricane Irma was threatening to go through Miami, from South to North, and cause havoc on more than three million inhabitants. Both the authorities and the media were considering it to be a destructive storm. There was an order of evacuation in almost every county.

Accessing the situation, as a priest, I activated our entire ministry in prayer. Several of my other sons and daughters around the world also joined us in prayer. During a final meeting with the ministry employees, I took authority in the spirit and declared in the name of Jesus that the hurricane would change direction and weaken; and, it was so. The moment Hurricane Irma touched Cuba, it changed directions instead of continuing North, as predicted, it moved West towards the Gulf of Mexico. When it finally went North, it passed far from Miami, with winds of only 115 mph (185 kph) and went down to a category three hurricane. Eventually, it became a tropical storm and weakened until it dissipated completely. God answered our prayers, and delivered us from what would have been a historical tragedy!

Declaring Upon the Nations:

RECENTLY I VISITED A region in Ethiopia called Addis Ababa. We went to take the supernatural power of God and to empower the body of Christ in that nation. In that time, the country was going through a challenging time in government, and the Lord gave me a prophetic word for them, in which He said: *"Ethiopia, I will raise a new government to do my will and bless my people. In the next few years you will see two different governments, and among them, I will raise a Christian. Ethiopia, you are my people; you have suffered greatly, but I have heard your cry. I will make a change in your economy. It will no longer be said about you that you are one of the poorest countries in the world because I will bring prosperity to this nation. The sign of this will be that I will raise young leaders, of the new wine, who will be on fire for My Spirit and My presence".*

During that trip, Apostle Tamrak, from Ethiopia, introduced me to one of his spiritual sons, a young politician who was running for the presidency. The Holy Spirit showed me that he was a crucial man for this country, and I felt to give him a prophetic word. On April 2nd of 2018, this young man, Dr. Abiy Ahmed, was sworn in as the first Christian Minister of Ethiopia. In his victory speech, he said that the transition was the beginning of a new political era for Ethiopia, which is called to become the first success economy in the East of Africa. I got to experience, first-hand, the prophetic word God had for Ethiopia come to life through the young priest, now, Minister of Ethiopia Dr. Ahmed.

5 | A Call to Holiness

THE FIRST SIGN that must distinguish the priesthood of the last days is holiness. Today, we don't frequently hear about holiness, not even in churches. While holiness is attainable, it is not something we can easily achieve, and therefore seeking it has been set to one side or even been given up on by many churches. As for those believers and church leaders who do speak about pursuing holiness they are often categorized as religious fanatics and rejected. Nevertheless, the Bible categorically states that *"God did not call us to uncleanness, but in holiness"* (1 Thessalonians 4:7) and urges us to pursue two things: *"peace with all people, and holiness, without which no one will see the Lord"* (Hebrews 12:14).

What does it mean to be "holy"? It doesn't mean that being perfect or never sinning. It means to be consecrated and separated for the exclusive use of God; to be cleansed and purified to remain without blemish or wrinkle. Holiness is the evidence of having been washed and cleansed by the sacrifice of Jesus and by God's Word, through the ministry of the Holy Spirit; it testifies of the "spiritual hygiene" of the believer. It is a state of constant purity and innocence. It is to be free of mixtures, impurities, and contamination. As Paul wrote, *"The God of peace Himself sanctify you completely; and may your whole spirit, soul, and body be preserved blameless at the coming of our Lord Jesus Christ"* (1 Thessalonians 5:23).

The Bible compares the church's holiness in relation to Christ to the holiness that should be nurtured and preserved in the marriage relationship: *"Husbands, love your wives, just as Christ also loved the church and gave Himself for her, that He might sanctify and cleanse her with the washing of water by the word, that He might present her to Himself a glorious church, not having spot or wrinkle or any such thing, but that she should be holy and without blemish"* (Ephesians 5:25-27).

Agents of Holiness

We should continuously seek after holiness. However, by our flawed human nature, the ability to be holy does not exist; it isn't something we can achieve on our own merits or do in our own strength; but God, who is holy, provides us with three agents that produce holiness. If we want to live holy, we must take the initiative to sanctify ourselves through the Word, the blood of Christ, and the Holy Spirit.

- ### The Word

    When we are saved, we are removed from the cycle of sin, and God gives us new and eternal life. Our whole lives need to reflect the holiness of our renewed spirits. We are sanctified by God's Word, which gives life to everything that was dead because of sin. For that reason, we must not reject the Word, because we run the risk of not being cleansed. It is important to meditate on the Word of God at all times. Likewise, it is important that we don't abandon the commandments and advice contained therein. Knowing this, the psalmist said: *"How can a young man cleanse his way? By taking heed according to Your word. With my whole heart I have sought You; Oh, let me not wander from Your commandments! Your word I have hidden in my heart, That I might not sin against You. Blessed are You, O Lord! Teach me Your statutes"* (Psalms 119:9-12).

- ### The Blood of Christ

    The blood of the Lamb that is without blemish and without spot, who is Christ Jesus, cleanses us from all sin. No work we do can free us from the guilt of sin, *"but if we walk in the light as He is in the light, we have fellowship with one another, and the blood of Jesus Christ His Son cleanses us from all sin"* (1 John 1:7). This means that the blood cleanses us when we repent and confess our sins, as we apply the work of Christ on the cross to our life.

> *The blood cleanses us of sin and the Word cleanses us from corruption.*

- **The Holy Spirit**

   The Holy Spirit, sent to us by Christ, is the One who purifies us. This purification is symbolized by these elements with which the Spirit is identified: water, fire, and wind. He cleanses all the impurities in our life; He takes away the iniquity that comes through our bloodline as generational sin, and He delivers us from all spiritual bondage that leads us to sin.

In the course of our daily lives, we are exposed to many different people, situations, and places, and if we are not on guard, contamination can enter our lives through our senses and emotions. Such contamination can fill us with bitterness, false doctrines, and immorality. Hence, we need the continual cleansing provided by these three agents that God has provided for us: The Word, the blood of Christ, and the Holy Spirit.

Stages of Consecration and Separation

There are three stages that we must go through to achieve our total consecration to God. These can't be done all at once, because the process requires revelation, denial of self, surrender to God, and maturity. These stages are:

- **Separating Ourselves from Everything That Is Not Beneficial**

   The first thing that God does when He wants to consecrate us exclusively for Him is to draw us apart from the world (worldliness), the flesh, unhealthy relationships, and other negative influences, soul ties, and environments that are not beneficial to us. That is, God separates us from things that contaminate our soul or mind. For example, worldly music tends to cause depression or to push people to sin and violence. God separates us from false ideologies and cultures, and anything else that separates us from Him.

He also distances us from the desires of the flesh that contaminate our body, for example, sexual immorality. He draws us away from relationships that separate us from Him. He breaks harmful soul ties because, for example, if we have a lack of forgiveness from past relationships, this will prevent us from surrendering completely to Christ. This also includes friends who do not want to surrender their lives to Christ, and even Christian friends who don't want to commit themselves to God or His Kingdom.

He also separates us from other attachments, such as hobbies that take away the time that God wants us to dedicate to Him. Finally, God separates us from toxic places, like jobs at businesses that use illegal practices or lie for profit. He might also cause us to move to another city or country to take us where our call will develop or manifest. It is important that we are attentive to God's demands and not resist them. Everything that God takes away from our life is for the purpose of drawing us closer to Him and fulfilling His will, which is always good, acceptable, and perfect. (See Romans 12:2.)

> **When God wants us for Himself, He separates us from everything that separates us from Him.**

■ Consecrating Ourselves to God

To consecrate ourselves is to dedicate ourselves in spirit, soul, and body—with a total and absolute commitment—to something or someone. Earlier, I spoke about how the Levites of the Old Testament were consecrated. They led a totally different life from the rest of the people. God did not assign them land, but each tribe gave them cities from their territories, because the Levites' inheritance was the Lord and His presence. Neither did the Levites dedicate themselves to multiplying livestock or crops, but only to minister to the Lord at the altar, praising God with their instruments, studying the Scriptures and teaching them to the people, guarding the doors of the temple, and welcoming the people to represent them before God, among other important functions.

Our consecration to God must be in alignment with the call we have. If you have been called to one of the fivefold ministries of Ephesians 4:11, or a business person who is called to invest in the kingdom's expansion, the time will come when your dedication to the ministry and God's purpose for your life will be full-time. Then the time will also come when God will sustain you economically, and you will be able to bless others! However, if we are attached to things, possessions, people, or activities that take us away from God, our consecration is not complete. God demands total consecration and surrender, just as He gave Himself completely to us in the person of Jesus Christ.

> **To consecrate ourselves is to dedicate ourselves completely to fulfill the purpose and the calling of God.**

■ Consecrating Ourselves to a Purpose and a Calling

The consecration to a purpose is the total and absolute dedication to what God has called us to do. That dedication, in holiness and total commitment, is what will allow us to see the passion that God put in our hearts be fulfilled. For example, I was called to bring the supernatural power of God to this generation, and since the day I received that revelation, I have devoted myself entirely to fulfill it; I have sanctified, separated, and consecrated myself to fulfill that purpose.

Everything I do has to do with that calling. I pray, fast, study the Word, and seek fresh revelation of the Holy Spirit; I run risks of all kinds for the sake of the kingdom; I let the blood, the Word, and the Spirit cleanse and purify me every day; I train people based on the vision that God has given me, so that they take supernatural power to more people, more cities, and more nations; I record my teaching and preaching for others to hear, write books, compose songs, record television and radio programs, and much more. In everything I do, I manifest the supernatural power of the God who saves, heals, performs miracles, transforms lives, raises the dead, frees the captive, and establishes His kingdom on earth. I live consecrated to the purpose that God deposited in me—and I fulfill it in His way, not mine.

The weight of the presence of God in a person comes from their consecration.

If you consecrate yourself to God's purpose, you will witness how God will use you to bring changes in people, cities, and countries. Those who do not cleanse and consecrate themselves completely will never fulfill their calling; and what they do will always be contaminated with that from which they have not been cleansed. This is how the mixtures of spirits that are so harmful in the church are produced. Unfortunately, this generation is taking lightly what God does; therefore, if you are part of the remnant, your consecration is imperative, and it must be greater each day. Only in this way can you manifest that you walk with God and have a relationship with Him, and that you do not take His work and His calling for your life lightly.

The Line of Holiness

Today, it is often difficult to recognize the difference between Christians and unbelievers, since the line that should separate them—that of holiness —is increasingly thin. The church, in its desire to be accepted by modern society, has given up values, relaxed morals, ignored the demand for holiness, and lowered the standard of separation and consecration. I continue to believe and preach that there must be a clear line that divides the believer from the unbeliever, to mark the difference between holiness and sinfulness. Someone who has not separated themselves for God is just like anyone else; they cannot be light to the world, nor can they represent Christ.

> **The line of holiness differentiates the consecrated believer from the so-called one; the light of those who are consecrated must shine in the midst of darkness.**

The Mark of the Remnant is Holiness

God's character has many wonderful qualities, but His primary mark or identifier is holiness. He is holy. God cannot be compared to anyone else. Nobody is like Him! Our God is different from all "gods." He is in another category altogether. *"Who is like You, O Lord, among the gods? Who is like You, glorious in holiness, fearful in praises, doing wonders?"* (Exodus 15:11). The primary quality that makes God different is holiness.

Currently, in our society, there are two types of churches growing hand in hand: one with natural interests, which adapt to the demands of those who are deciding where to attend church; and the other, which is the holy and supernatural church, the church of Christ. The former has not been transformed; it still wears the garments of sin, and in order to grow, it does not care about compromising the truth or holiness, so it can keep the membership happy and not unbalance its budget. The latter, however, lives in constant spiritual transformation, walks from glory to glory, and always seeks to live separated, sanctified, and consecrated to God; moreover, its growth is linked to the second coming of the Lord.

> **The transformation of the church occurs by becoming the bride of Christ, through holiness.**

Final Word for the Remnant

If God is holy, the church must be holy. We cannot put the church in the same category as anything else in the world, because if we did, it could not be holy (see Ephesians 5:26-31). The church is the body of Christ; it belongs to Him. Jesus is the manifestation of the *"the fullness of the Godhead bodily"* (Colossians 2:9). If anyone denies that Jesus is a man, as well as God, this is from the spirit of the antichrist. (See, for example, 1 John 4:2; 2 John 1:7.) Jesus is our example of who we should be: *"But as He who called you is holy, you also be holy in all your conduct, because it is written, 'Be holy, for I am holy'"* (1 Peter 1:15-16).

God calls us to be part of the holy priestly remnant. Everyone who belongs to Christ must separate themselves from the things, persons, and circumstances that separate them from God, to consecrate themselves completely to Him. Jesus is calling the church, corporately, to resume its priestly function; this includes separation and consecration to a life of righteousness and holiness. This church that is pure, clean, without spot and without wrinkle, is the one that He will take with Him at His second coming. Therefore, the line that separates the believer from the rest of the world must be radical. The Scripture presents it in this way: *"He who is unjust, let him be unjust still; he who is filthy, let him be filthy still; he who is righteous, let him be righteous still; he who is holy, let him be holy still"* (Revelation 22:11). Let us dedicate ourselves to being holy at the time of His coming!

> *When people resist change, they worsen;*
> *that is a sign of the judgment of God.*

ACTIVATION:

I wanted to leave this chapter until the end because I feel Christ is placing a stronger demand on His church in the last days; many men and women of God agree it has intensified. I feel this demand in my spirit very strongly, and I think the restoration of our priesthood is the only way to be ready to face the coming times, and to discern the coming of the Lord. The priesthood is crucial in the preparation of the church for the return of our Savior. If you love God and want to do what God is demanding from you to do as part of the remnant that is watching for the coming of the King of Kings, you must sanctify and consecrate yourself to God. Join me and thousands of other priests who are reading this book right now, and let's pray together:

"Beloved Heavenly Father, through these pages, I have received in my heart the demand from the Holy Spirit to be the priest that that You need me to be in this time we're living in. I don't want to remain on the sidelines, asleep, entertained with the world or satisfying the desires of the flesh. I want to separate from everything that draws me away from You and consecrate myself permanently for You and the purpose you have determined for my life. I want to cross the line that leads me to holiness, and allow Your blood, Your Word and Your Spirit to cleanse me from all sin, all impurity, all devious desire and all distraction. I want to consecrate myself to You; I want You to be able to count on me, on my prayers, spiritual sacrifices, worship, offerings, righteous acts, and everything else that Jesus showed us. Cleanse me, wash me, purify me in Your presence. Separate me for Your exclusive use. Fill me with Your Spirit and power and activate my priesthood. Lead me to be a carrier of Your presence, to manifest Your power and love to this world, and to be an agent of change for my family, and for everyone around me. Here I am! I answer this call to holiness and I make a decision to consecrate myself for You, by Your grace. I pray in the name of Jesus. Amen!"

TESTIMONIES

Pastor Josue Salcedo has a powerful testimony of how, over eight years he consecrated himself more and more to God, and how this led him to become passionate about His presence and about being that priest that Jesus wants all men to be:

"I was raised in the church, but it was a powerless church. I grew up knowing I had to go to Sunday school; but there came a time when I started to rebel and to want to know the world. For seven years of my life I was in the world, involved in gangs, looking for money, in clubs, parties, drinking and illicit relationships. I had never had an encounter with God, so I decided to seek answers in other options. My father had started to attend King Jesus church, and, one day, he invited me to a deliverance retreat. Once there, the pastor who was preaching gave me a word of knowledge and told me things that only I knew. I started crying and I had an encounter with God. In the past, while I grew going to a church, I always battled between doing the things of God or losing myself in sin and in the world. There were times when I had encounters with God and I was in fire for Him, but that impartation and infilling lasted for only a moment and then it left. It was like that until I decided to discipline myself and consecrate. When I made the decision to know God, I could see the changes in my life. God told me I had to be available for Him and that, even if I made mistakes or ruin things, I had to get to church; even if I was tired or I didn't feel like going, I had to go. Then I saw that, the more I gave to God, and the more I sacrificed myself, the more my passion for Him grew. It was not anymore something that came and went; now it was a permanent passion.

"Since then, I became bold to evangelize wherever I go. I have preached in airplanes, buses, basketball games, schools, concerts and public events. I raised a House of Peace where up to sixty people would show up every week. As I consecrated myself to God, I allowed Him to mold me as a priest of His Kingdom; and to mold my character to submit to authority. Every time I have an encounter with God, I change, and I become more passionate about Him, and that passion leads me to serve Him more. My life was transformed by the sanctification and the consecration to God. Today I am an ordained Pastor and God uses me to minister miracles, deliverance and to preach the gospel wherever I go. Additionally, I train and disciple many people to lead them to consecrate to God and be transformed, just as I was".

THE FOLLOWING IS THE testimony of Manny, a young man who decided to consecrate his business to God, to give an unusual offering and in response he saw a supernatural miracle in his finances:

"I came because a friend brought me to this church. That day they were talking about CAP (the Conference of the Apostolic and the Prophetic, that King Jesus organizes every year). In that time, I was opening a business, and I felt from God that I had to be in that conference. The truth is that this church is supernatural. When I went to CAP, I saw things I had never seen before. Nothing was normal for me. The Apostles and pastors said God had told them to sow big. And I prayed to God: 'If it's You, confirm it to me in my spirit'. And He answered: 'Son, if he is distorting my Word I will deal with him, but you be obedient and sow'. So, I gave the biggest offering I have ever given in a church. I didn't do in my own will, but in obedience to God. My business was just starting, and that same day, the first day of CAP, we broke sales records; the second day of CAP, we broke sales records again; and then on the third day of CAP, we broke another record of sales. When I left CAP, I received an e-mail saying that my business was on second place on sales, among the businesses that had opened that week. And I said: 'God, we are number two, but your people are supposed to be number one!' In that same instant I received another e-mail telling me we were number one! My business is number one in sales among all the businesses that opened that day!"

PASTOR DANIEL TOMÁS, FROM Argentina (South America), has a powerful testimony of what it is to enter under the covering of a priesthood consecrated to God and how that affected his own priesthood and that of his church:

"My mane is Daniel Tomás, and I am the Pastor in a church in San Carlos de Bariloche, in the South area of Argentina. Our congregation was around two hundred people, there was a beautiful manifestation from God, but we were looking for something greater. We believed there was something more from the Lord we were missing.

One day, the book *'How to walk in the supernatural power of God'* written by Apostle Guillermo Maldonado; and that book revolutionized us. The priesthood in our church was awakened and we started seeking more from God in prayer. I started following Apostle Maldonado through internet, and when I saw the level of miracles that God did, I wanted to have that. I traveled to the United States and had an interview with the apostle to ask for spiritual covering. He was very kind with me and we were able to start the procedures to obtain the covering. That process lasted six months; but the moment we entered under the spiritual covering of King Jesus, and the spiritual fatherhood of the apostle, the power of God increased in our church. Rapidly, our membership went from two hundred to six hundred people.

"The miracles are something huge and they have revolutionized the neighborhood and the city; but what moves me the most is how my priesthood and the priesthood of the people have awakened. People started to consecrate and dedicate themselves more to God; we started moving in a different dimension of glory. With the growth of our priesthood (through the revelation contained in Apostle's books, his preaching and impartation) a greater dimension of miracles, growth and expansion came.

"We went from being a normal church to be a church lit in the fire of the Lord. People had gotten used to the services, the preaching, the liturgy, the music; and we were stuck. But when we entered under the covering of a house where the priesthood functions at a very high level, the church was activated; the youth went to the streets to preach, to pray for the people, and to see instantaneous miracles. It started a different dynamic of service and commitment. That was the key!

"Now, people have a different disposition to serve and to consecrate to the Lord. The church is committed with the vision and with growth; we are all under the same vision of expansion. Sometimes, we as pastors make the mistake of thinking that we have it all and that we don't need to expand. Then, we conform. However, I believe the key is to consecrate to God and, when we do, He shows us there is much more of His power that we haven't seen".

About the Author

Active in ministry for over twenty years, Apostle Guillermo Maldonado is the founder of King Jesus International Ministry—one of the fastest-growing multicultural churches in the United States—which has been recognized for its development of kingdom leaders and for visible manifestations of God's supernatural power.

Apostle Maldonado earned a master's degree in practical theology from Oral Roberts University and a doctorate in divinity from Vision International University. He gives spiritual coverage to 338 pastors and apostles of local and international churches in 50 countries, which form part of a growing association, the Network of the Supernatural Movement. Also, he is the founder of the University of the Supernatural Ministry (USM), which provides men and women with teaching, training, impartation, and activation, both in the Word and in the demonstration of God's supernatural power.

Some of his most recent books are: How to Walk in the Supernatural Power of God, The Glory of God, The Kingdom of Power, Supernatural Transformation, Supernatural Deliverance, Baptism in the Holy Spirit, and Divine Encounter with the Holy Spirit. In addition, he preaches the message of Jesus Christ and His redemptive power on his national and international television program, The Supernatural Now, which airs on TBN, Daystar, the Church Channel, and seventy other networks, thus with a potential outreach and impact to more than two billion people across the world.

Apostle Maldonado resides in Miami, Florida, with his wife and partner in ministry, Ana, and their two sons, Bryan and Ronald.

If this book is a blessing for you, your family or your ministry, we thank you for sending us your comments. If you have a testimony of what the power of God has done in your life, you can contact us at Phone 305-382-3171 or write to:
http//kingjesusministry.org/share

King Jesus International Ministry
14100 SW 144th Ave. Miami, FL 33186
Phone: 305.382.3171 - Fax: 305.382.3178
sales@kingjesusministry.org